AF225999

If 'They' Assassinate Him

IMRAN KHAN

The Last Hope

Leading the Change Amid Dark Forces

For a Self-Reliant, More Prosperous Pakistan

by, Faisal I. Siddiqi

SizLink
COMMUNICATIONS

If 'They' Assassinate Him,
Imran Khan – The Last Hope,
Leading The Change Amid Dark Forces

First Edition – October 2024

Author: Faisal I. Siddiqi
Published by: SizLink Communications
                1.855.749.5465

Library and Archives Cataloguing in Publication
information is available.

ISBN: 978-1-0691137-0-2

To my parents, whose wisdom and values taught me to stand firm in the face of adversity, always choosing what is right, I owe my deepest gratitude. Your guidance has shaped me into who I am today.

To my beloved wife, who has stood by me through every trial and triumph with unwavering support and love. Your strength and belief in me have been a constant source of inspiration.

To my siblings, for your encouragement and steadfast belief in my journey. Your support has always provided me with the courage to keep moving forward.

"

IT IS NOT THE DEFEAT THAT DESTROYS YOU, IT IS BEING DEMORALIZED BY DEFEAT THAT DESTROY YOU.

COMPROMISE FOR YOUR DREAM BUT NEVER COMPROMISE ON YOUR DREAM.

YOU ALL HAVE TO MAKE A NEW PAKISTAN. NAYA PAKISTAN IS NOT A SLOGAN - IT'S A BELIEF.

I FURTHER PROMISE YOU, THAT ALL MY WEALTH AND PROPERTY WILL BE IN PAKISTAN. I WILL TAKE OWNERSHIP OF THIS COUNTRY AND WON'T BE LIKE THOSE LEADERS WHO CREATE HIDEOUTS ABROAD.

— Imran Khan

What Readers Are Saying

Riaz Qamar Siddiqi,

Energy & Asset Management Executive
Houston, Texas, USA

The book "If 'They' Assassinate Him, Imran Khan - The Last Hope, Leading The Change Amid Dark Forces" by Faisal I. Siddiqi delves into the life and political career of Imran Khan, chronicling his journey from a celebrated cricket icon to the political leader of Pakistan. The narrative highlights his transformation into a symbol of hope, resilience, and integrity, focusing on his efforts to fight corruption and advocate for justice. The book emphasizes Khan's ambition to build a "Naya Pakistan" (New Pakistan) and the challenges he faced, particularly from entrenched political and military powers that resisted his reform agenda.

Key sections of the book to explore:

1. Imran Khan's Early Life and Cricket Career: His leadership of Pakistan's cricket team to a World Cup victory in 1992 set the stage for his later political career, showing his ability to inspire and lead.

2. Philanthropy: Khan's dedication to building the Shaukat Khanum Memorial Cancer Hospital and Namal University showcased his commitment to Pakistan's welfare, which endeared him to many.

3. Political Struggles: The book traces his political rise, from the founding of Pakistan Tehreek-e-Insaf (PTI) in 1996 to his eventual victory in the 2018 general election. It discusses his focus on anti-corruption and his reformist agenda, while also highlighting the opposition and military interference that led to his ousting in 2022.

4. Post-Power Struggles: Following his removal from office, Khan continued to rally his supporters, fighting against what he called a corrupt and manipulated system. The book also touches on assassination attempts and his imprisonment in 2023, portraying him as a resilient leader determined to return to power.

5. Impact on the Muslim World: Khan's advocacy for Muslim causes, such as his stance on Kashmir and Palestine, his fight against Islamophobia, and his push for greater unity among Muslim nations, are explored in depth.

The book concludes with reflections on Imran Khan's lasting influence on Pakistan's political landscape and the broader Muslim world, framing him as the last hope for meaningful reform in the country.

Syed F.H. Burney,

Corporate Executive & Entrepreneur
Sr. Political Analyst

As someone who spent a significant part of my career navigating the corporate landscape in Pakistan, I have witnessed how leadership can either propel or dismantle a vision. Reading this comprehensive account of Imran Khan's life and political journey served as a powerful reminder of how one man's resolve can shape a nation.

The author skillfully captures the essence of Khan's transformation from a celebrated sportsman into a political figure striving for national reform. The book dives into his unwavering determination to address a system plagued by corruption and inefficiency. What resonated with me the most was how the narrative illuminated Imran's internal struggles, the personal sacrifices he endured, and his relentless pursuit to challenge the status quo.

I commend the author for presenting a nuanced, thought-provoking account that offers readers valuable insights into both Khan's leadership and the broader socio-political landscape of Pakistan.

Latafat Ali Siddiqui,
Sr. Journalist, Author and
Chief Editor, Canadian Asian News

Having interacted with both Faisal Siddiqi and Imran Khan over many years, I find this book to be an insightful and balanced portrayal of Khan's journey. My relationship with Khan goes back to his cricketing days, and I had the opportunity to interview him during his early years of philanthropy while I was with Arab News in Jeddah—I documented in my own book. While I have often been critical of Khan's policies and political decisions, there is no denying the impact he has had on Pakistan's political and social landscape.

Faisal skillfully captures Khan's transformation from a revered sportsman to a polarizing political figure. The narrative reflects an intimate understanding of the man behind the public persona, portraying both his resilience and his vulnerabilities. What makes this book stand out is its objective approach: Faisal does not attempt to whitewash Khan's controversial decisions or policies. Instead, he offers a thorough examination of both the triumphs and setbacks Khan has faced in his career.

While I may not agree with many of Khan's policies, particularly in the political realm, I appreciate how this book provides a well-rounded view of his evolution. Faisal's understanding of Pakistan's governance system, combined with his global perspective, offers readers a unique window into the challenges Khan encountered in his shift from sports to politics.

This book is an important contribution to the ongoing discourse around Imran Khan's legacy, and while my critiques remain, I commend Faisal for his meticulous and balanced approach to telling this complex story.

Javed Ali Khan,
Sr. Corporate Banker (R)-(BCCI)
Montreal, Canada

I have had the privilege of knowing Imran Khan both personally and professionally during my time in Abu Dhabi while working for BCCI (Bank of Credit and Commerce International). Our paths crossed several times, and I had the unique opportunity to witness Khan's integrity and honesty firsthand.

As someone who has observed him up close, I can attest that his commitment to fighting corruption and creating a just society stems from genuine personal convictions. These values were not political rhetoric for him; they were principles he lived by, as I saw during our interactions. His honesty was, and continues to be, one of his most defining traits, something I have always admired and respected.

Even as I fight my own battle with acute cancer, my support for Khan has never wavered. His determination and resilience, especially in the face of such immense challenges, have only strengthened my belief in him. Despite my health struggles, I continue to stand with him because I know his leadership is grounded in the same ideals he lived by years ago—integrity, honesty, and an unwavering commitment to a better Pakistan, (qualities I've witnessed firsthand, and they continue to inspire me).

This book captures the essence of Khan's relentless fight for a just and fair Pakistan, values I know he has always stood by.

Contents

What Readers Are Saying v

Prologue - Tumultuous journey 1

From Cricket to Adiala Jail – The Journey of Imran Khan 3

A Genuine Case Study of a Real Brand - Rise of a Star and Leader 13

Imran Khan's as Prime Minister of Pakistan 20

Imran Khan's Impact on the Muslim World 33

Khan's Speech At The United Nations 39

Khan's Achievements in Power 42

Imran Khan's Ouster in 2022:   The Controversial No-
Confidence Vote 48

2023 Elections – The Biggest Fraud in Pakistan's History 54

The Unwavering Support for Imran Khan Post-2023 Fraudulent Election
.... 64

Why Imran Khan Was Removed? 70

India and the U.S. Involvement in Pakistan's Power Game 76

Pakistan's Resources Under Siege by Corrupt Military and Political
Pundits 82

Economic Hit Man: Pakistan as a Clear Example 89

Awakening of Public Consciousness and Unprecedented Support for

Khan 92

The Unbroken Spirit of Resistance 100

Asim's Assault on Democracy and the Military 106

Asim Munir at a crossroads with Imran Khan 113

The Fight for Democracy–The Fight for Pakistan 119

If Military Dare to Assassinate Khan - Directly or Indirectly? 125

Course Correction: The Only Option for the Military 132

How Global Powers Stand to Gain from Imran Khan's Return 139

Moving Forward: Imran Khan-The Only and Last Hope to Make

Pakistan a Great Country 145

Prologue - Tumultuous journey

Pakistan's political landscape has always been one of intrigue, power struggles, and external manipulation. The rise of Imran Khan, a former cricket star turned politician, ushered in a new chapter in the nation's history, promising hope and reform. His vision for a "Naya Pakistan" (New Pakistan) and relentless fight against corruption captured the imagination of millions, propelling him to power in 2018 and placing him at the forefront of the nation's quest for justice, accountability, and progress.

This book explores the tumultuous political journey of Imran Khan, from his meteoric rise to his controversial ousting and the possibility of his return. It delves into the key events that shaped his time in power, including his efforts to tackle Pakistan's deep-seated corruption, revive its economy, and navigate the treacherous waters of international diplomacy.

At the heart of this story lies a persistent theme: the battle between entrenched power structures—military elites, corrupt politicians, and foreign actors—and a leader determined to bring change. The chapters detail how these forces have consistently aligned against Khan, from rigged elections to international conspiracies, to prevent his reforms from taking root.

Khan's journey has not only been a political one but also a personal struggle for survival. In the last three years, he has survived multiple assassination attempts, underscoring the extreme lengths to which his opponents have gone to silence him. These attempts on his life have only galvanized his resolve, reinforcing his image as a leader willing to risk everything for the future of Pakistan. Each attack has deepened the polarization within the country, as his supporters see him as a lone warrior battling a corrupt system, while his critics accuse him of fueling division.

While many of Khan's opponents accuse him of populism and eroding democratic norms, his supporters argue that his mission is a necessary correction to decades of mismanagement and exploitation. His fight was never just against corruption; it was against a system designed to serve the few at the expense of the many. Khan's return to power, should it come to pass, represents not only the re-emergence of a political figure but a reckoning for all who have benefited from Pakistan's broken system.

This book aims to provide a comprehensive account of Imran Khan's political journey, the forces aligned against him, and the potential implications of his return. It also seeks to offer a deeper understanding of the broader context—domestic and international—that has shaped Pakistan's tumultuous political landscape. Khan's story is one of resilience, but it is also the story of a nation at a crossroads, struggling to define its future in the face of internal challenges and external pressures.

As Pakistan moves forward, the questions raised in these pages are more relevant than ever: Will Khan's return mark a new era of reform and accountability? Or will the corrupt forces and international players thwart his vision yet again? The answers to these questions will shape Pakistan's destiny in the years to come.

From Cricket to Adiala Jail – The Journey of Imran Khan

Many books have been written about Imran Khan, a man whose life has been marked by remarkable achievements and extraordinary challenges. His story is one of transformation, from a celebrated cricketer and philanthropist to one of Pakistan's most inspirational and followed political leaders. From the fields of international cricket to the solitary confinement of Adiala Jail, Imran Khan's journey is a testament to his unwavering passion, determination, and commitment to his country.

1. Early Life: The Making of a Leader

Born on October 5, 1952, in Lahore, Pakistan, Imran Khan belonged to a privileged but deeply rooted Pashtun family. From an early age, Khan displayed the traits of a leader. He was educated at Aitchison College, Lahore's most prestigious school, before attending the Royal Grammar School in England and later enrolling at Keble College, Oxford, where he earned a degree in Philosophy, Politics, and Economics. It was during his time in England that Khan's skills as a cricketer began to shine, propelling him to international fame.

2. The Cricket Star: Leading Pakistan to Glory

Imran Khan's cricket career is legendary. Known for his elegant yet aggressive playing style, he became one of the world's most celebrated all-rounders. But it was his leadership of the Pakistan cricket team that would secure his place in history. In 1992, Khan led Pakistan to its first-ever Cricket World Cup victory, a moment that remains etched in the nation's memory. His  cricketing success made him a national hero and cemented his status as a global icon.

His leadership on the field, characterized by resilience, confidence, and the ability to inspire his teammates, foreshadowed his future political career. Even in moments of adversity, Khan's determination to lead by example made him stand out. His World Cup triumph became a metaphor for his later political life—a testament to the idea that greatness is achieved through perseverance and belief in oneself.

3. The Philanthropist: Passion for Pakistan

After retiring from cricket, Imran Khan did not fade from public view. Instead, he embarked on an entirely new journey—one of philanthropy and nation-building. His greatest philanthropic achievement came with the establishment of the **Shaukat Khanum Memorial Cancer Hospital & Research Centre** in Lahore, named after his mother who died of cancer. The hospital was the first of its kind in Pakistan, providing world-class care to thousands of patients, regardless of their ability to pay.

Khan's passion for helping the underprivileged extended to education as well, with the creation of **Namal University** in Mianwali. Both institutions reflect his long-standing commitment to giving back to his country and providing opportunities to those who might not otherwise have them. Khan's philanthropy endeared him to millions, furthering his reputation as someone who cared deeply for the welfare of Pakistan's people.

4. The Loved Celebrity: Charisma and Global Appeal

Imran Khan's charisma was not confined to cricket or philanthropy. He was one of the few Pakistani figures who transcended borders, becoming a global celebrity with admirers worldwide. His good looks, combined with his intellect and leadership qualities, made him a favorite of the international media.

His high-profile marriage to **Jemima Goldsmith**, a British socialite, further enhanced his global image, though it also exposed him to intense public scrutiny. Throughout the 1980s and 1990s, Khan was a fixture in international

society—a man who could effortlessly move between the worlds of sport, philanthropy, and celebrity. Yet, despite his success and acclaim, he never lost sight of his true calling: to bring meaningful change to Pakistan.

5. Spiritual Journey: Sufism, Quran and Prophet's Guidance

Imran Khan's interest in Sufism is closely tied to his deep desire to understand the Quran and his strong adherence to the teachings of Prophet Muhammad (PBUH) and his Seerat (life and character). Khan has often expressed how his spiritual journey has been shaped by a profound connection to Islamic principles, with a particular focus on the Quran's guidance for leading a just and moral life. **His respect for the Prophet's teachings is evident in his repeated references to the Prophet's example of leadership, compassion, and justice**. Khan's political manifesto reflects this spiritual alignment, as he began with the verse from the Quran,

"Eeyaka Na'budo wa Eeyaka Nastayeen"
("You alone we worship, and You alone we ask for help"), signaling his reliance on divine guidance in his mission. His approach to governance, rooted in the principles of humility, service, and moral integrity, is a reflection of his dedication to following the Quran and the Seerat of the Prophet, which aligns closely with the Sufi emphasis on self-purification and spiritual enlightenment. His spiritual influence has not only resonated with Muslims but has also inspired many non-Muslims to explore Islam, with some even embracing the faith after being drawn to its message of peace and selflessness, which Khan often emphasizes. For instance, Christina Baker, a former journalist, publicly credited Imran Khan's influence in inspiring her to learn about Islam. After reading more deeply into the

teachings of Islam, she eventually converted to the faith, becoming one of the notable examples of how his message transcends religious boundaries and promotes a deeper understanding of Islam's universal values.

6. The Inspirational Leader: The Birth of a Political Icon

In 1996, Imran Khan founded the Pakistan Tehreek-e-Insaf (PTI), a political party dedicated to fighting corruption and advocating for justice and accountability in Pakistan. Khan entered politics not as a traditional politician but as a reformer determined to break the status quo. His vision of a ***"Naya Pakistan"*** (New Pakistan) resonated with the masses, especially the youth, who saw in him a leader untainted by the corruption and dynastic politics that had long plagued the country.

However, the road to political success was fraught with

challenges. Khan's initial foray into politics was met with failure, as PTI struggled to gain a foothold in Pakistan's entrenched political system. But his determination, much like in his cricket career, never wavered. Over the years, Khan built PTI into a formidable political force, gaining traction with his anti-corruption rhetoric and commitment to transparency and good governance.

In the 2018 general elections, Imran Khan's perseverance paid off when PTI won a historic victory, and **Khan was sworn in as Prime Minister of Pakistan**. This moment marked the culmination of his years of relentless struggle against corruption, injustice, and political elites. His government embarked on ambitious reforms, from healthcare to education, while launching various initiatives aimed at improving the lives of the poor and marginalized. Under his leadership, projects like Ehsaas, aimed at alleviating poverty, and Sehat Insaf Cards, designed to provide free healthcare to millions, were introduced, reflecting his deep commitment to social welfare.

However, despite the success of PTI, it became widely known that even in the 2018 elections, the military establishment allegedly engineered the results to deny PTI a supermajority in parliament. Around 30 seats were reportedly manipulated to ensure that PTI would only have a simple majority, thereby limiting Khan's control and forcing him to rely on coalition partners. This act of political engineering was seen by many as a deliberate attempt to curb Khan's authority and prevent him from fully implementing his reform agenda.

7. The Downfall: Political Engineering and Khan's Imprisonment

As Khan's political career reached new heights, it also attracted powerful enemies. His refusal to align with the corrupt elites and his pushback against foreign influence led to increasing tensions with the military establishment and other entrenched interests. His stance on an independent foreign policy, especially his refusal to bow to foreign pressures—famously captured in his defiant phrase **"Absolutely Not"**—set him on a collision course with Pakistan's powerful military and political figures.

In April 2022, Imran Khan's government was ousted through a controversial no-confidence vote, an event many believe was orchestrated by both domestic power players and foreign interests. Undeterred, Khan launched a massive resistance movement, traveling across the country to gather support and rally his base against what he called the imported government.

But Khan's resistance would lead to his imprisonment. In August 2023, he was arrested and placed in Adiala Jail, charged with politically motivated offenses designed to silence him. **His imprisonment, in solitary confinement and subjected to mental torture, marks the most difficult chapter of his life. Yet, despite the regime's attempts to break his spirit, Khan remains a beacon of hope for millions of Pakistanis who continue to rally for his release.**

8. Imran Khan: The People's Leader

Despite the trials and tribulations, Imran Khan remains a symbol of resistance and hope. To his supporters, Khan is the only leader who can restore Pakistan's dignity and sovereignty. He is seen as a man who has sacrificed everything — his family, fame, fortune, and personal freedom — for the sake of his country.

Khan's indomitable spirit has become an inspiration for those who believe in the dream of a Naya Pakistan—a nation free from corruption,

exploitation, and foreign domination. His journey from the cricket fields to Adiala Jail mirrors the struggle of a nation searching for its identity, its freedom, and its future.

9. From Cricket to Solitary Confinement

Imran Khan's life is a story of transformation—from a celebrated cricketer to an imprisoned political leader who continues to fight for justice and change. His journey from the

world of sports to the harsh reality of solitary confinement in Adiala Jail represents the ultimate sacrifice of a man who, against all odds, refuses to give up on his vision for Pakistan.

As he endures mental and physical hardship in confinement, the people of Pakistan await his return, believing that Imran Khan is still the hope they need to lead them toward a brighter and more just future. His love for Pakistan, his passion for justice, and his unyielding commitment to his principles ensure that his legacy will endure, no matter the obstacles. Imran Khan's journey is far from over, and for millions, his release represents the first step toward realizing the dream of a truly free and democratic Pakistan.

10. Bid to run for Chancellor of Oxford University

Imran Khan's bid to run for Chancellor of Oxford University in 2024 comes after the resignation of Chris Patten, marking Khan's first attempt at the prestigious role. Having previously served as Chancellor of the University of Bradford between 2005 and 2014, Khan brings extensive experience in academic leadership. Known for his philanthropic work, particularly in healthcare through the Shaukat Khanum Cancer Hospital, and his global recognition as a cricket legend, Khan's campaign centers on enhancing Oxford's role in global collaboration, sustainability, and inclusivity. His candidacy holds symbolic importance for Pakistan and the broader South Asian community, reflecting how global figures from diverse backgrounds can leave a lasting impact on one of the world's most prestigious universities.

IMRAN KHAN

A Genuine Case Study of a Real Brand - Rise of a Star and Leader

Imran Khan's journey from a celebrated sports icon to a powerful political figure is not just the story of a man—it is the making of a brand. He has transcended the realms of sports, philanthropy, and politics to become a symbol of hope, resilience, and integrity. Today, his name resonates with millions of people in Pakistan and around the world. From the cricket pitch to political rallies, Khan has built an identity that inspires deep loyalty, admiration, and unwavering support. This chapter explores how Imran Khan evolved into a genuine brand, capturing the hearts and minds of millions.

From a branding perspective, Imran Khan's influence in Pakistan is so powerful that his name alone carries immense weight in the political landscape. His personal brand, built over decades through his cricket legacy, philanthropic efforts, and political leadership, resonates deeply with his supporters. It's often said that in a fair election, the strength of his brand is such that even if he were to assign an election ticket to a 'pole,' it would secure a victory with a significant margin. This reflects the loyalty and trust that his followers place in him, underscoring the sheer impact of his persona in shaping electoral outcomes.

1. Building the Foundation: The Rise of a Sports Legend

Imran Khan's brand began on the cricket field. Known for his distinctive playing style, Khan quickly became a global cricketing superstar in the 1970s and 1980s. His leadership qualities shone through early in his career, culminating in the historic 1992 Cricket World Cup victory. His ability to inspire, lead, and perform under pressure was instrumental in creating a heroic image that transcended the boundaries of sport.

Khan wasn't just a cricketer; he was a national icon. His image as a gentleman athlete—one who played with grace, determination, and fair play—solidified his standing as a symbol of Pakistan's potential on the world stage. The World Cup victory became more than just a sporting triumph; it became a metaphor for Khan's ability to unite and uplift a fractured and skeptical nation.

2. The Transformation into a Philanthropist

A defining element of any successful brand is its alignment with a higher purpose. For Imran Khan, this alignment came through his philanthropic work. After the death of his mother from cancer, Khan embarked on one of the most ambitious projects in Pakistan's history—building the **Shaukat Khanum Memorial Cancer Hospital & Research Centre**. What seemed like an impossible dream became a reality due to his tireless efforts and crowdsourced support from Pakistanis at home and abroad.

Khan's work in philanthropy, including the creation of **Namal University** in his hometown of Mianwali, gave him a moral authority that went beyond his fame as a cricketer. He was now seen as a man of deep compassion, committed to giving back to society. These initiatives were key in

shaping Khan's brand as a humanitarian, further endearing him to the masses.

3. Crafting the Political Leader

When Imran Khan transitioned into politics by founding the Pakistan Tehreek-e-Insaf (PTI) in 1996, he was already a celebrated figure. However, turning his personal charisma and popularity into a political brand was no easy task. Khan's early years in politics were difficult. His party struggled to gain traction, and his stance against corruption and elite politics made him many enemies.

But Khan's authenticity, a crucial element of his personal brand, never wavered. His message of justice, accountability, and self-reliance resonated deeply with younger generations and the disenfranchised. He positioned himself as an outsider—a politician who would challenge the status quo. This was key to building a brand of leadership that differentiated him from the traditional power players in Pakistan, known for dynastic politics and entrenched corruption.

Khan's anti-corruption rhetoric, combined with his straight-talking style and independent vision, set him apart as a man of principles—someone who refused to compromise on his ideals. This allowed him to slowly but surely cultivate a base of passionate supporters, particularly among the youth, who saw in Khan the leader they had been waiting for.

4. The Pivot: "Naya Pakistan" and Political Breakthrough

The pivotal moment in Khan's political career came with his 2018 general election victory, where his vision of **"Naya Pakistan"** (New Pakistan) resonated across the nation. His brand had finally come to full fruition. His platform emphasized transparency, social justice, education, and an independent foreign policy—promises that captured the imagination of a country weary of the traditional ruling elite.

In Khan, people saw a man who represented honesty and patriotism, untainted by the cronyism that plagued Pakistan's politics. His image as a reformer was the core of his political brand, and it was this authenticity that led him to victory. Despite challenges and criticism, Khan positioned himself as a leader who would bring hope and renewal to Pakistan.

His rise to power was not just the ascent of a politician; it was the rise of a brand built on trust and integrity. The slogan **"Tabdeeli"** (Change) became synonymous with his political identity, a rallying cry for those who believed in his promise of a new, better Pakistan.

5. Imran Khan: A Brand of Resilience and Defiance

One of the most significant elements of Imran Khan's brand has been his resilience. Over the years, Khan has faced enormous political and personal challenges—from being ousted from power in April 2022 through a controversial no-confidence vote to enduring imprisonment in Adiala Jail. Yet, his brand has remained strong, even growing in popularity during his time behind bars.

Khan's ability to withstand adversity and stand up for his beliefs has become central to his identity. His phrase "Absolutely Not," rejecting foreign interference, particularly from the U.S., in Pakistan's domestic and foreign affairs, became a powerful slogan that solidified his position as a nationalist leader willing to stand up to global powers. His defiance against the military establishment and the political elite has only enhanced his image as a leader who fights for sovereignty and independence.

Even in jail, Khan's brand has not diminished. If anything, his imprisonment has turned him into a martyr figure, galvanizing public support and further entrenching his position as Pakistan's last hope. His supporters, often described as a movement, remain loyal, seeing in Khan the embodiment of their desire for justice, accountability, and self-determination.

6. A Personal Brand that Transcends Politics

Imran Khan's personal brand transcends his political career. As a cricketer, philanthropist, and politician, he has cultivated an image based on integrity, strength, and a commitment to

Pakistan's well-being. His life is viewed as a genuine case study in personal branding, where authenticity, purpose, and resilience have played critical roles.

Unlike many other leaders, Khan's brand has remained consistent across the various phases of his life. Whether leading Pakistan to victory in the 1992 World Cup, building a cancer hospital, or leading political rallies, he has always positioned himself as a man of the people—someone who represents hope in the face of adversity. This consistency has earned him trust and loyalty from his supporters.

His ability to inspire across generations and classes—whether young people seeking change or the rural poor yearning for justice—demonstrates the power of his brand. Imran Khan is not just a politician; he is a living symbol of what many Pakistanis believe their country can become.

7. A Genuine Case Study of a Real Brand

Imran Khan's journey from sports star to national leader is the epitome of a genuine, evolving brand. He has leveraged his early success as a cricketer and philanthropist to build a political identity grounded in integrity, authenticity, and resilience. Despite facing overwhelming challenges, Khan's brand remains unshaken—a testament to his deep connection with the people of Pakistan.

Today, Khan represents more than a political figure—he is the face of hope for millions who see in him a leader who stands for justice, honesty, and sovereignty. His brand, built over decades, has solidified him as not just a leader but a symbol of resistance and a rallying cry for change.

Imran Khan's story is a real case study of a man who has turned his life into a powerful brand that continues to inspire and lead, even in the most challenging of circumstances. From cricket fields to political imprisonment, Khan's brand reflects the hopes and aspirations of a nation in search of a better future

.

Imran Khan's as Prime Minister of Pakistan

Imran Khan's tenure as the 22nd Prime Minister of Pakistan, from 2018 to 2022, was marked by a distinctive blend of ambitious reforms, profound challenges, and an unyielding drive to change the political and economic landscape of the country. Khan's government was driven by a vision of a "Naya Pakistan" (New Pakistan), aimed at establishing a welfare state, reducing corruption, and addressing the economic woes that had plagued Pakistan for decades. However, his time in office also encountered significant obstacles, both internal and external, which would ultimately impact his political career and the future trajectory of the country.

Key Achievements of Imran Khan's Tenure

1. Economic Reforms and Public Confidence

One of the most significant achievements of Imran Khan's tenure was his focus on stabilizing Pakistan's economy, which was grappling with a widening fiscal deficit, low foreign exchange reserves, and rising inflation. Despite these challenges, Khan's government managed to restore some degree of economic stability, thanks largely to public confidence in his leadership.

Economic Growth and GDP Performance (2021-2022): The Pakistan government reported an impressive GDP growth rate of 5.97% for the fiscal year 2021-22, surpassing earlier projections. This growth was largely driven by the industrial and agricultural sectors, alongside a surge in exports and remittances. The government's ability to stimulate key sectors during a period of global economic uncertainty helped stabilize the economy temporarily.

Foreign Exchange Reserves: Under Khan's leadership, Pakistan saw an increase in foreign exchange reserves, which were bolstered by the confidence of overseas Pakistanis. This confidence manifested in the form of remittances through the Roshan Digital Account, a ground-breaking initiative that allowed overseas Pakistanis to send money back home securely and efficiently. The initiative not only boosted the economy but also made it easier for overseas Pakistanis to invest in Pakistan's real estate, equities, and other sectors.

Remittances Growth: The inflow of remittances saw an all-time high, totaling around $31.2 billion for the fiscal year 2021-22, marking a remarkable 9.6% increase compared to the previous year. This was one of the major drivers of Pakistan's foreign exchange reserves and contributed significantly to stabilizing the national economy during a time of crisis.

Highest Ever Exports: Perhaps one of the most notable successes during Imran Khan's leadership was the record-breaking surge in Pakistan's exports. Under his government, the country observed its highest-ever exports in history, with a total export value of $31.8 billion for FY 2021-22. This remarkable achievement reflected growing confidence in Pakistan's industrial and manufacturing sectors. Policies such as tax incentives, subsidies, and the reduction of red tape played a crucial role in encouraging export-oriented industries like textiles, rice, and electronics to flourish.

2. Overseas Remittances via Roshan Digital Accounts

The Roshan Digital Accounts (RDA) became a vital tool for Pakistan's economic recovery, especially at a time when the country faced increasing foreign debt. The accounts facilitated seamless banking transactions for Pakistanis abroad, enabling them to send remittances back to Pakistan with greater ease. This initiative not only provided Pakistan with a reliable foreign exchange inflow but also strengthened the connection between the country and its diaspora. By the end of 2021, the Roshan Digital Accounts had attracted billions of dollars in deposits and investments from Pakistanis living abroad, marking a historic milestone for Pakistan's financial sector.

3. Social Welfare Programs

Khan's government introduced an array of social welfare programs, the most prominent being the **Ehsaas Program**, which aimed to provide financial assistance to the country's poorest and most vulnerable citizens. The program's sub-components, including **Ehsaas Kafaalat, Ehsaas Nashonuma, and Ehsaas Undergraduate Scholarships**, focused on tackling poverty, malnutrition, and improving educational opportunities for deserving students.

Ehsaas Kafaalat provided financial aid to widows and impoverished families, ensuring a basic income for the most disadvantaged groups. Ehsaas Nashonuma focused on tackling malnutrition in women and children, while Ehsaas Undergraduate Scholarships enabled students from low-income families to pursue higher education.

Additionally, Khan introduced the **Insaaf Sehat Card**, which aimed to provide healthcare insurance to millions of Pakistanis, ensuring access to medical care for those unable to afford it. This initiative was particularly beneficial in a country where healthcare has traditionally been a luxury reserved for the affluent.

4. Pandemic Response – Smart Lockdowns

Imran Khan's leadership during the COVID-19 pandemic earned Pakistan recognition globally. Under his direction, Pakistan implemented a smart lockdown strategy that allowed the country to minimize the economic fallout while controlling the spread of the virus. This approach focused on targeted lockdowns and maintaining essential services, rather than imposing widespread, blanket shutdowns, which could have crippled the economy. Pakistan's COVID-19 response was praised internationally, and the country was ranked as the third-best performing nation in handling the pandemic. The government's swift actions, including the distribution of food and financial aid to vulnerable populations, helped mitigate the crisis.

5. Foreign Policy Achievements

Khan's tenure also saw significant strides in Pakistan's foreign policy. Khan emphasized an independent foreign policy, prioritizing Pakistan's sovereignty over foreign pressures. Under his leadership, Pakistan made efforts to improve its relations with neighboring countries, particularly India, despite challenges in the relationship. Khan also succeeded in restoring Pakistan's credibility on the global stage, particularly in the context of advocating for Muslim causes, such as the plight of the Rohingya Muslims in Myanmar and the Kashmir issue with India.

Khan's government played an important role in facilitating dialogue between Afghanistan's Taliban leadership and the international community, contributing to Pakistan's position as a central player in regional geopolitics.

6. Educational Reforms: A New Curriculum for Bridging Class Divides

One of the hallmark reforms of Imran Khan's government was the introduction of a Single National Curriculum (SNC), aimed at reducing educational disparity between the elite and the general populace. The previous education system in Pakistan was fragmented, with private schools offering curricula often disconnected from the public sector's offerings. This system resulted in significant disparities in educational outcomes, with the elite receiving a superior education, often abroad, while the lower-income segments had limited access to quality education.

Imran Khan's vision was to create a more egalitarian education system, one that would bridge the divide between the upper and lower classes. The SNC aimed to standardize education across the country, ensuring that every child, regardless of their background, would receive the same quality of education. By introducing a unified curriculum, the government sought to reduce the divide between different social classes and promote social cohesion.

One of the significant aspects of the SNC was the inclusion of Islamic Studies, including the Quran and Seerat-un-Nabi (Prophet's Life), as integral components of the curriculum. These subjects were not only designed to provide spiritual guidance but also to foster moral values and social responsibility in students. The inclusion of these subjects was seen as a step towards building a society grounded in ethical principles, which was crucial for Khan's vision of creating a "welfare state" based on Islamic values.

The implementation of the Single National Curriculum and the incorporation of Islamic teachings are expected to have profound, long-term effects on Pakistani society. By ensuring that all children, regardless of their socio-economic background, receive the same foundational education, Khan aimed to foster a more inclusive society. Over time, these reforms could contribute to reducing class-based divisions, promoting equal opportunities, and creating a more equitable and cohesive national identity.

7. Sustainability and Youth Empowerment

Another important initiative under Khan's government was the focus on youth empowerment. Recognizing that Pakistan has one of the youngest populations in the world, Khan introduced initiatives aimed at equipping the youth with the skills and opportunities necessary to drive the country's future growth. These included youth entrepreneurship programs, skill development initiatives, and vocational training designed to prepare young people for the job market.

Moreover, Khan's government aimed to harness the potential of Pakistan's young population in the global economy by focusing on digital literacy and access to online learning platforms. This would allow the youth to not only participate in the national economy but also engage in global opportunities.

Key Challenges Faced by Imran Khan's Government

Despite these achievements, Khan's government faced several major challenges, many of which hindered his ability to fully realize his vision for a "Naya Pakistan."

1. Economic Instability and Inflation

While Khan's economic reforms brought some positive outcomes, Pakistan's economy continued to face major difficulties. High inflation, a widening fiscal deficit, and persistent unemployment plagued the nation. Khan's promises to stabilize the economy were often overshadowed by the realities of a global recession exacerbated by the COVID-19 pandemic.

The cost of living in Pakistan rose sharply, and the government's failure to effectively address inflation, especially in food and fuel prices, led to public frustration. Despite his efforts to seek loans from international institutions like the IMF, the economic situation remained precarious, contributing to growing discontent.

2. Political Opposition and Media Criticism

Khan's government faced fierce opposition from political rivals, particularly the Pakistan Peoples Party (PPP) and Pakistan Muslim League-Nawaz (PML-N). These parties criticized his leadership and blamed him for Pakistan's economic troubles, arguing that his government failed to deliver on key promises. They capitalized on public dissatisfaction, particularly with the economic situation, which led to a significant decline in public support for his government.

Additionally, Khan's relationship with the media was tense. His government frequently clashed with media outlets, accusing them of bias and attempting to discredit his administration. Critics argued that Khan sought to suppress free speech, which led to allegations of authoritarianism during his tenure.

3. Healthcare and Education Challenges

Despite the introduction of the Insaaf Sehat Card and the Ehsaas Program, healthcare and education remained areas of significant concern. Pakistan's healthcare infrastructure struggled to meet the demands of a growing population, and the quality of education remained subpar, particularly in rural areas. While Khan's government made strides in improving these sectors, the impact was often limited by systemic inefficiencies and underfunding. While the Insaaf Sehat Card aimed to provide free health insurance to millions, the healthcare system as a whole still faced significant challenges, including inadequate facilities and a shortage of skilled medical professionals. Similarly, the Single National Curriculum was a step in the right direction for educational reform, but its full implementation across the country encountered resistance from various provincial governments, limiting its immediate effectiveness.

4. Governance and continued corruption

Khan's anti-corruption rhetoric was one of the central themes of his political campaign. However, his efforts to address corruption faced significant hurdles. The National Accountability Bureau (NAB), an anti-corruption body that Khan's government empowered, made several high-profile arrests of opposition leaders and government officials, but critics argued that these actions were politically motivated. Khan's government was also accused of failing to bring about systemic reforms that would address the root causes of corruption. Although the rhetoric was strong, the actual implementation of anti-corruption measures remained a work in progress, often bogged down by institutional resistance and political opposition.

5. Foreign Policy Complications

On the foreign policy front, while Khan was successful in forging stronger ties with several countries and advocating for the rights of Muslims globally, his tenure also witnessed tensions with key partners. Relations with the United States and other Western countries were often strained due to Khan's independent stance on issues like Afghanistan and Kashmir, where his government advocated for a more assertive position. Pakistan's relationship with India, particularly regarding

Kashmir, remained volatile, and the diplomatic isolation in the aftermath of the revocation of Article 370 by India was a significant issue during his tenure.

While Khan sought to mediate peace and stability in Afghanistan, Pakistan's involvement in the region often led to internal debates, especially when the Taliban returned to power. These geopolitical complexities posed challenges for Pakistan's foreign policy and its relations with key international stakeholders.

6. Opposition to Electoral Reforms and the Battle for Fair Elections

Imran Khan's demand for electronic voting was a bold step aimed at ensuring fairness and transparency in Pakistan's electoral process, which has long been marred by allegations of manipulation and rigging. Khan believed that implementing electronic voting would significantly reduce opportunities for fraud, bringing legitimacy to elections. However, this move faced strong opposition from General Bajwa and the power circles within the establishment, who preferred to maintain the status quo of election engineering they had grown accustomed to. These forces resisted the reforms, knowing that transparent and fair elections would diminish their ability to influence outcomes. Beyond direct rigging, **"ghost voters"**—fictitious or deceased individuals still listed on voter rolls—play a crucial role in the establishment's manipulation of election results. By inflating voter numbers and controlling ballots cast in the names of these ghost voters, the establishment can sway results in their favor, undermining the democratic process. Another significant challenge Khan faced was the refusal of power circles to grant the right of voting to overseas Pakistanis, a move he strongly supported. Millions of Pakistanis abroad, who contribute substantially to the economy through remittances, were denied their constitutional right to participate in elections. Khan's push for both electronic voting and overseas voting threatened to dismantle these tactics, which is why they were met with such resistance from those who benefit from electoral manipulation.

Legacy of Imran Khan

Despite the challenges, Imran Khan's tenure as Prime Minister is marked by several long-lasting achievements that will impact Pakistan for years to come.

During his time in government, Imran Khan focused on addressing the fundamental, deep-rooted issues facing Pakistan, rather than pursuing short-term, populist measures aimed at winning immediate political gains. His vision was to create sustainable, long-lasting change by targeting the structural problems that had hindered the country's development for decades. Khan's policies centered around reforming critical sectors like education, healthcare, and social welfare, and he initiated programs such as the Ehsaas Program to alleviate poverty and provide support to the most vulnerable. He also worked on building a transparent and accountable governance system, combating corruption, and introducing reforms in taxation and public services. His approach was rooted in a belief that by fixing the core issues—inequality, lack of opportunity, and governance failures—Pakistan could achieve true progress and development, even if these efforts required time and were not immediately politically popular. This long-term vision distinguishes his legacy from leaders who focused solely on short-term political victories, positioning his tenure as an effort to fundamentally reshape the future of the nation.

His economic reforms, social welfare programs, and efforts to tackle corruption marked a significant shift in Pakistan's governance model. The introduction of the Roshan Digital Accounts, Ehsaas Program, and the Insaaf Sehat Card are reforms that continue to provide benefits to millions of Pakistanis. The Single National Curriculum, with its focus on education and Islamic values, could have a profound, positive effect on Pakistan's future, by ensuring that all students, regardless of their socio-economic background, have access to the same quality of education.

Khan's advocacy for a "Naya Pakistan" helped reshape the national discourse around corruption, governance, and social welfare. His commitment to improving the lives of ordinary Pakistanis and providing a safety net for the most vulnerable was evident through his social welfare initiatives, which have set a foundation for future governments to build upon.

However, Khan's tenure also revealed the immense challenges of governing a country like Pakistan, with its complex political, economic, and social landscape. The persistent issues of economic instability, political opposition, and corruption highlighted the difficulty in translating ambitious reforms into lasting change. His government's inability to fully address these challenges, coupled with the growing frustration among the public, contributed to his eventual ousting from power.

Despite the setbacks, Imran Khan's political journey has left an indelible mark on Pakistan's history. His tenure was a period of significant reform, as well as a reminder of the complexities and challenges involved in leading a nation striving to navigate its way through socio-political and economic turmoil. His legacy, much like his leadership, will continue to be a subject of debate and analysis for years to come.

In conclusion, while Imran Khan's time in power was fraught with both remarkable achievements and major obstacles, it was a period of transformation that set the stage for Pakistan's future. The policies he introduced, particularly in the realms of social welfare, economic reform, and education, have had a lasting impact. The challenges he faced, particularly in terms of political opposition, economic instability, and institutional resistance, reflect the complexities of governance in Pakistan. Regardless of the political changes that may follow, Khan's tenure stands as a testament to the determination to bring about change in a country that has long struggled with issues of governance, corruption, and socio-economic inequality

Imran Khan's Impact on the Muslim World

Imran Khan's tenure as Pakistan's Prime Minister not only reshaped his country's political and economic landscape but also had a far-reaching impact on the broader Muslim world. Khan emerged as a prominent Muslim leader, advocating for key issues affecting the Ummah (global Muslim community) and taking bold stances on international platforms. His leadership was defined by his vocal opposition to Islamophobia, his defense of oppressed Muslim communities, and his consistent push for unity among Muslim-majority countries. Central to this was his principled stance on contentious issues like the Kashmir conflict, Palestine, and, notably, his firm position on Israel.

1. A Voice Against Islamophobia

One of the hallmarks of Imran Khan's leadership was his unwavering campaign against Islamophobia. As anti-Muslim sentiments rose globally, particularly in the West, Khan positioned himself as a defender of Muslim rights and worked to combat misconceptions about Islam. He frequently condemned the media's tendency to associate Islam with extremism and violence, and he actively sought to change the global narrative around the religion.

Khan was especially vocal on international platforms, including the United Nations, where he called out world leaders and media organizations for spreading negative stereotypes about Muslims.

He pushed for a global initiative to combat Islamophobia, proposing an international day to raise awareness about the issue and advocating for legal measures to protect Muslims from hate speech and discrimination.

His leadership on this issue resonated deeply with Muslims around the world, especially in Europe and North America, where Islamophobia had become a pressing concern. Khan's willingness to speak openly and forcefully about this issue made him a leading voice in the Muslim world, inspiring both leaders and ordinary citizens to stand against religious intolerance.

2. Advocating for Palestine and Kashmir

Imran Khan's tenure was also marked by his strong advocacy for two of the most significant and longstanding issues affecting the Muslim world: the Palestinian cause and the Kashmir dispute.

On Palestine, Khan's government maintained Pakistan's traditional stance of unwavering support for the rights of the Palestinian people and their quest for an independent state. He consistently called for a two-state solution based on pre-1967 borders, as outlined by various UN resolutions, and condemned Israeli policies in the occupied territories. Khan did not shy away from criticizing Israel's actions, particularly its military offensives in Gaza and its expansion of settlements in the West Bank.

Khan's stance on Israel was unequivocal: he firmly opposed the normalization of relations between Pakistan and Israel as long as the Palestinian issue remained unresolved. He refused to bow to international pressure, especially from some Arab and

Western countries, to recognize Israel, insisting that Pakistan would not abandon the Palestinian cause. Khan often framed the issue as one of justice, declaring that Pakistan could not compromise on its moral and ethical obligations to stand with the oppressed. His refusal to engage with Israel earned him respect and admiration in the Muslim world, where many saw him as a leader who upheld principles over political expediency.

Khan's stance on Kashmir was similarly forceful. After India's controversial revocation of Article 370 in August 2019, which stripped Jammu and Kashmir of its special status, Khan became the most vocal advocate for the Kashmiri people's right to self-determination. He condemned India's actions as illegal and inhumane, highlighting the human rights abuses in the region and calling for global intervention. His speeches at the UN were particularly powerful, where he equated the situation in Kashmir with the struggles of other oppressed Muslim populations and warned of the potential for conflict between two nuclear-armed neighbors.

3. Khan's Firm Stance on Israel

Imran Khan's position on Israel remained one of the most defining elements of his foreign policy, especially in the context of the broader Muslim world. Despite a global trend toward the normalization of ties with Israel, particularly among Arab nations through agreements like the Abraham Accords, Khan stood his ground, maintaining Pakistan's historical opposition to formal relations with Israel.

Khan repeatedly emphasized that Pakistan would not recognize Israel unless there was a just resolution to the Palestinian issue, stating, "Our stance is clear: unless the Palestinians get their due rights and a just settlement, Pakistan cannot recognize Israel." This position resonated with many in the Muslim world, particularly those who were disillusioned by the growing number of Arab countries normalizing relations with Israel despite the continued occupation of Palestinian territories.

Khan saw the Palestinian struggle as a symbol of resistance against colonialism and oppression, and his refusal to compromise on this issue was a reflection of his broader commitment to justice for oppressed peoples. His stance also echoed Pakistan's founding principles, as its first leader, Muhammad Ali Jinnah, had also opposed any recognition of Israel without a fair resolution for Palestinians.

Khan's firm position on Israel earned him widespread support among ordinary Muslims, particularly in countries where pro-Palestinian sentiment runs deep. However, it also put him at odds with some Western governments and a few Gulf nations that had shifted toward engagement with Israel. Despite this, Khan remained resolute, prioritizing moral integrity over geopolitical gains.

4. Building Unity Among Muslim Nations

Imran Khan consistently sought to promote greater unity among Muslim-majority countries, particularly through forums like the Organisation of Islamic Cooperation (OIC). He believed that the Muslim world could only address its myriad challenges—including poverty, conflict, and external interference—through cooperation and solidarity.

Khan advocated for stronger ties among Muslim nations, urging them to work together on economic, political, and security matters. He often highlighted the importance of intra-Muslim trade and investment as a means to reduce dependence on Western economies and foster self-reliance within the Muslim world. Khan's vision included promoting collaboration in science, technology, and education to uplift the Muslim world's economic and intellectual capabilities.

Though his efforts at building Muslim unity were constrained by the geopolitical realities of the region—such as the rivalry between Saudi Arabia and Iran—Khan remained committed to the idea that the Muslim world could emerge as a powerful, independent bloc if it stood united. His efforts to mediate tensions between Iran and Saudi Arabia during his tenure reflected his broader goal of preventing conflict within the Muslim world and promoting harmony among its nations.

5. Challenges and Limitations

Despite his best efforts, Imran Khan's influence in the Muslim world faced several challenges. The deep political and sectarian divisions between key Muslim-majority countries, particularly between Sunni and Shia blocs, limited his ability to foster the kind of unity he envisioned. The economic and political dependencies of many Muslim countries on Western and Gulf powers also constrained their ability to collaborate independently on global Muslim issues.

Moreover, while Khan's stance on Israel and Palestine earned him respect in many quarters, it also isolated Pakistan from some potential diplomatic and economic opportunities, particularly as more countries began normalizing relations with Israel. However, Khan's firm refusal to engage with Israel was seen as a testament to his commitment to moral and ethical principles, even when it meant going against the tide of international diplomacy.

6. A Lasting Legacy in the Muslim World

Imran Khan's leadership left a lasting impact on the Muslim world, particularly in his advocacy for justice, unity, and the protection of Muslim rights. His principled stance on Israel, his outspoken defense of Kashmir, and his efforts to combat Islamophobia positioned him as a leader willing to stand up for the global Muslim community, even when it was unpopular or politically risky to do so.

While his broader vision of Muslim unity remained unrealized, his legacy as a defender of Muslim causes endures. Khan's tenure as Pakistan's Prime Minister marked a period of renewed activism on issues of deep significance to Muslims worldwide, and his voice on global platforms echoed the sentiments of millions who felt marginalized or oppressed.

For many, Imran Khan represented a beacon of hope—a leader who dared to challenge the status quo, stand against injustice, and champion the rights of the Ummah. His impact on the Muslim world may continue to inspire future leaders to take up the mantle of justice and unity for the betterment of all Muslim nations.

Khan's Speech At The United Nations

Imran Khan's speech at the United Nations General Assembly in September 2019 became a defining moment in his political career and in Pakistan's foreign policy. His address, which garnered widespread attention, not only captured the imagination of Pakistanis but also resonated globally, breaking records for the most-watched speech by any leader on United Nation's YouTube channel.

Khan's impassioned speech, delivered with unwavering conviction, focused on four major themes:

1. **Kashmir Conflict:** He raised the issue of the Kashmir region, emphasizing India's revocation of Article 370 and the subsequent lockdown in Indian-administered Kashmir. Khan called attention to human rights violations and warned of potential conflict between two nuclear-armed nations.

2. **Islamophobia:** Khan addressed the rise of Islamophobia around the world, calling for global efforts to combat hatred and misunderstanding toward Muslims. He linked this to the

broader war on terror and how it has fueled negative stereotypes about Islam.

3. **Climate Change:** He highlighted the urgent need for action on climate change, referencing Pakistan's vulnerability to environmental disasters and urging the international community to take concrete steps to mitigate its impact.

4. **Corruption and Money Laundering:** Khan also discussed the negative impact of corruption and illicit financial flows from developing countries to rich nations, stressing the importance of addressing this global issue to reduce poverty and economic inequality.

These themes showcased Pakistan's pressing concerns while reflecting broader global issues.

One of the key moments in the speech was his critique of the international community's double standards, especially regarding its treatment of Muslim-majority countries. Khan highlighted the rising tide of Islamophobia across the globe and the marginalization of Muslim communities, stressing that the world needed to recognize the injustices faced by Muslims, including the situation in Palestine and the growing discrimination against them in Western countries.

In addition to his defense of Muslim causes, Khan also raised concerns about the growing environmental challenges, stressing the need for global cooperation to address climate change. He emphasized Pakistan's efforts to combat environmental degradation, notably through the country's ambitious tree plantation campaign.

The speech, marked by its clarity, sincerity, and boldness, garnered millions of views on YouTube, setting a new benchmark for political speeches in the digital age. It was widely praised for its diplomatic tone, yet unapologetic stance on issues that had long been ignored or underrepresented on the global stage.

Khan's United Nations speech marked a turning point in his leadership, as it showcased his ability to stand firm on global issues while representing Pakistan's interests with dignity and assertiveness. It also solidified his position as a leader who was willing to speak truth to power, regardless of the political or diplomatic ramifications. The speech remains a symbol of his vision for a more just, equitable, and peaceful world.

Khan's Achievements in Power

Imran Khan's tenure as Prime Minister of Pakistan (2018-2022) was marked by significant achievements, particularly in the areas of economic reform, social welfare, and governance. Despite facing immense challenges, including a global pandemic, political opposition, and external pressures, Khan's government made noteworthy strides in several sectors. His policies reflected his vision for a "Naya Pakistan"—a nation self-reliant, transparent, and economically resilient.

Imran Khan's key achievements, focusing on the economic growth Pakistan witnessed under his leadership, even as the world was gripped by the COVID-19 pandemic. It will also explore how these successes may have drawn negative attention from international establishments, which, some argue, sought to stymie Pakistan's growth for geopolitical reasons.

1. Stabilizing a Fragile Economy: Turning Crisis into Opportunity

When Imran Khan took office in 2018, Pakistan was grappling with an economic crisis. The country's external debt was soaring, foreign reserves were depleting, and inflation was rising sharply. Khan inherited a fragile economy, burdened by years of mismanagement and corruption. One of his first priorities was to stabilize the economy, which required difficult decisions, including seeking financial assistance from international lenders like the International Monetary Fund (IMF).

Despite criticism for turning to the IMF, Khan's government managed to negotiate a bailout package that came with stringent economic reforms. These reforms, though tough in the short term, laid the foundation for long-term financial stability. Under his leadership, Pakistan improved its fiscal discipline, brought down the current account deficit, and increased foreign reserves. By 2021, Pakistan's economy had begun to stabilize, and growth projections looked promising.

2. Economic Growth Amid the Global COVID-19 Pandemic

One of the most remarkable achievements of Khan's government was its handling of the economy during the COVID-19 pandemic. While the global economy contracted sharply, Pakistan managed to not only survive the crisis but also register growth during one of the most challenging periods in modern history.

The government implemented a well-coordinated response to the pandemic, balancing health concerns with economic needs. Khan resisted calls for prolonged nationwide lockdowns, which helped keep the economy afloat, especially for daily wage earners and small businesses. Instead, his government introduced "smart lockdowns," which targeted specific areas with high infection rates while allowing most of the country to continue functioning.

Under Khan's leadership, Pakistan's economy grew by 3.94% in 2020-21, defying predictions of a severe recession. Pakistan was one of the few countries to achieve positive economic growth during the pandemic. Key sectors, such as construction and agriculture, were given special incentives to keep operations going, while Khan's flagship social welfare program, the Ehsaas Program, provided direct financial assistance to the poorest segments of society.

3. Social Welfare: The Ehsaas Program

One of Imran Khan's most celebrated achievements was the launch of the Ehsaas Program, the largest social welfare initiative in Pakistan's history. The program was designed to provide financial assistance to millions of underprivileged Pakistanis, addressing poverty, hunger, and unemployment.

The program gained international recognition for its transparency and effectiveness. It included cash transfers, scholarships for students, interest-free loans for small businesses, and shelter homes for the homeless. The Ehsaas Emergency Cash Program, introduced during the COVID-19 pandemic, was a lifeline for millions of families, distributing over $1.2 billion to the most vulnerable households.

By the time Khan left office, the Ehsaas Program had become a cornerstone of his government's efforts to build a more equitable society. It was a tangible manifestation of his vision for a welfare state, where the government played an active role in protecting the most vulnerable segments of society.

4. Boosting Exports and Strengthening Key Industries

Under Imran Khan, Pakistan made significant progress in increasing its exports, particularly in the textile, agriculture, and IT sectors. His government introduced policies to enhance production and competitiveness in key industries, leading to an increase in the country's export revenue.

The textile industry, a major contributor to Pakistan's economy, saw significant growth during Khan's tenure. By providing energy subsidies and other incentives, the government helped the sector recover from years of stagnation. Similarly, agricultural reforms, such as the Kamyab Kisan Program, aimed at modernizing farming practices, resulted in increased crop production and better yields.

Additionally, the IT sector became a rising star under Khan's government. Pakistan's tech industry grew rapidly, with a sharp increase in IT exports. Startups flourished, and the government's focus on digitization helped position Pakistan as an emerging tech hub in South Asia.

5. Tackling Corruption and Institutional Reforms

Khan's anti-corruption platform was central to his political ideology, and during his time in power, he took several steps to tackle the deep-rooted problem of corruption in Pakistan. His government launched investigations into financial irregularities, particularly those involving previous governments, and introduced reforms to increase transparency in public institutions.

One of the key reforms was the strengthening of the National Accountability Bureau (NAB), which played an active role in investigating high-profile cases of corruption. Although his critics accused him of political witch-hunting, Khan maintained that accountability was essential for building public trust and ensuring that state resources were used for the benefit of the people.

In addition to anti-corruption efforts, Khan's government introduced digital governance initiatives to make public services more efficient and accessible. Programs like Digital Pakistan aimed to digitize various aspects of governance, reducing bureaucratic inefficiencies and cutting down opportunities for corruption.

6. International Relations: Advancing Pakistan's Global Standing

Khan's leadership also saw Pakistan's growing importance on the global stage. His government adopted a foreign policy focused on improving relations with neighboring countries, particularly in areas of trade and economic cooperation. Khan played a key role in de-escalating tensions between Pakistan and India in 2019, following a military standoff, which showcased his diplomatic acumen.

Moreover, Khan's consistent advocacy for addressing climate change earned Pakistan international recognition. Under his leadership, Pakistan launched the Ten Billion Tree Tsunami project, one of the largest reforestation efforts in the world. This initiative not only contributed to environmental protection but also helped Pakistan enhance its standing in global climate forums.

7. Why the International Establishment May Have Targeted Pakistan's Growth

As Pakistan began to achieve economic success under Imran Khan, there were increasing concerns about external forces undermining these efforts. Some analysts argue that the international establishment, particularly certain Western powers, may have viewed Pakistan's growing self-reliance and economic progress as a threat to their geopolitical interests in the region.

Khan's focus on building an independent economic framework, reducing reliance on international loans, and fostering closer ties with non-Western powers like China and Russia may have disrupted the status quo. Moreover, his push for a more just global economic order, as well as his critiques of international financial institutions, might have put him at odds with powerful international actors.

This narrative gained traction as Khan's government was abruptly ousted in 2022, and subsequent political instability raised questions about the true motivations behind his removal. Many of Khan's supporters believe that external forces, fearing Pakistan's potential rise as an independent economic power, played a role in destabilizing his government.

A Legacy of Resilience and Progress

Imran Khan's tenure as Prime Minister was marked by resilience in the face of adversity and significant progress in economic and social development. Despite the many challenges, including a global pandemic, his government managed to stabilize Pakistan's economy, introduce ground-breaking social welfare programs, and put the country on a path toward self-reliance.

Khan's achievements, especially in the realm of economic growth and welfare, will likely be remembered as key milestones in Pakistan's recent history. Even though his time in power was cut short, the policies and reforms he implemented have left a lasting impact, demonstrating that with the right leadership, Pakistan can overcome even the most daunting challenges.

Imran Khan's Ouster in 2022: The Controversial No-Confidence Vote

In April 2022, Imran Khan, who had risen to prominence as the charismatic leader of the Pakistan Tehreek-e-Insaf (PTI) party, was ousted from power in a highly controversial and unprecedented no-confidence vote. This event marked a dramatic turning point in Pakistan's political history, one that continues to stir debate and has significant ramifications on the country's political landscape.

The Build-Up to the Vote

Imran Khan's government had been facing increasing pressure from the opposition, which included the Pakistan Peoples Party (PPP), Pakistan Muslim League-Nawaz (PML-N), and other smaller parties. The opposition accused Khan's administration of mismanaging the economy, failing to control inflation, and being unable to deliver on promises of governance reforms. However, these grievances were only part of the story.

What truly fueled the opposition's determination to remove Khan was his increasingly strained relations with Pakistan's military establishment and his foreign policy stance. Khan's independent foreign policy, especially his refusal to align with Western powers and his emphasis on sovereignty, particularly during the Ukraine war and his outspoken stance on the United States, irritated both domestic and international power centers.

Additionally, Khan's government had initiated anti-corruption investigations targeting his political opponents, which escalated tensions. The opposition parties saw an opportunity to unite and challenge Khan's rule, leading them to bring forward the no-confidence motion.

The Role of the Military: An Unseen Hand

One of the most significant aspects of Khan's ouster was the role of the military. Historically, the Pakistan military has wielded considerable influence over the country's political landscape, and this time was no different. Despite the fact that opposition parties such as PML-N and PPP had long been political rivals and bitter enemies, they were brought together by military generals to form an alliance aimed at ousting Khan. This unprecedented coalition, which defied longstanding political rivalries, raised suspicions about the military's hand in orchestrating the no-confidence motion.

The military establishment, led by General Qamar Bajwa and then by General Asim Munir, was believed to have played a decisive role in not just bringing these disparate political forces together but also in manipulating the political dynamics to ensure Khan's removal. While public rhetoric suggested that the opposition's unity was based on their shared opposition to Khan's leadership, the internal dynamics indicated that the military's covert intervention had played a crucial part in the coalition's formation.

This unnatural alliance was further solidified when, during the voting process, military officials allegedly ensured the passage of the vote of confidence. The opposition was seen to gain the upper hand, despite internal divisions within their ranks, which further fueled the belief that the military was behind the scenes ensuring a favorable outcome for the anti-Khan coalition.

The Dramatic Day: April 10, 2022

The no-confidence motion was presented in the National Assembly, with opposition parties accusing Imran Khan of incompetence and misrule. Khan, on the other hand, argued that his government was the target of a foreign conspiracy, a claim he reiterated in multiple speeches leading up to the vote. He believed that his removal was orchestrated by foreign powers, particularly the United States, who he alleged wanted to punish him for his independent foreign policy and refusal to bend to their will.

As the no-confidence vote proceeded, Khan made one last attempt to rally his supporters. He called for protests and rallies across the country, urging his followers to stand with him against what he called a "foreign-backed conspiracy." His message resonated with millions of Pakistanis, who viewed him as the symbol of change and a voice against political dynasties.

However, despite Khan's public pleas and calls for unity, the vote proceeded, and Imran Khan lost his majority in the assembly. On April 10, 2022, Imran Khan became Pakistan's first prime minister to be ousted through a no-confidence vote. The vote, which passed by a majority, saw 174 votes in favor of the motion, a clear sign of opposition unity.

The Aftermath: Allegations of Foreign and Military Conspiracy

Following his ouster, Khan's claims of a foreign conspiracy gained considerable traction, particularly within his party and supporters. Khan alleged that the United States, due to his independent foreign policy, had conspired with Pakistan's political and military establishment to remove him from power. This narrative found a receptive audience, especially among those who believed that Khan's administration was sabotaged by both internal and external actors.

The U.S. denied these allegations, calling them baseless. However, the controversy surrounding the vote continued to brew, and Khan's accusations of interference fueled growing distrust of the political system. Many of his supporters felt that the political elite, including former Prime Minister Nawaz Sharif and Asif Ali Zardari, had conspired against him, using the opposition's unity as a vehicle to remove him from power.

At the same time, the role of the military in orchestrating the no-confidence vote became more pronounced. Despite denials from the military, the widespread perception was that it had manipulated the vote outcome and influenced the decision-making of key players. The military's involvement, either directly or indirectly, in ensuring Khan's ouster deepened the rift between Khan and the powerful institution, with many of his supporters accusing the military of engineering a coup.

Public Reaction and Political Polarization

The news of Khan's ouster led to widespread protests, particularly from his loyalist base, which viewed his removal as an unjust act. PTI supporters flooded the streets, calling for immediate new elections and decrying the alleged conspiracy that had led to Khan's downfall. These protests, which continued for weeks, were marked by a sense of defiance and anger, with many participants claiming that the will of the people had been undermined by corrupt political forces.

Imran Khan, ever the charismatic leader, addressed his supporters, maintaining his stance on the foreign conspiracy and emphasizing that the fight for Pakistan's sovereignty was far from over. He called on his followers to take to the streets to demand accountability and justice.

The polarization in Pakistan's political landscape deepened, with Khan's supporters viewing his ouster as a democratic setback orchestrated by external forces. On the other hand, his opponents argued that Khan had failed in governance and that the no-confidence motion was a legitimate democratic process.

Imran Khan's removal from office in 2022 marked a pivotal moment in Pakistan's political history. Whether or not his claims of foreign interference were valid, Khan's ouster exposed deep flaws in Pakistan's political and institutional framework. His time in office, while marked by significant social welfare programs, economic challenges, and foreign policy achievements, also highlighted the underlying power struggles that exist within the country's political system.

The Interim Government: A Shield for Corruption Under the PDM's Umbrella

The creation of an interim government in Pakistan, particularly in the lead-up to elections, has always been a subject of significant debate and controversy. The interim setup is constitutionally mandated to ensure neutrality and fairness during the election process, but in the case of the 2023 elections, the composition of the interim government became a focal point of criticism, especially from the supporters of Pakistan Tehreek-e-Insaf (PTI) and its leader, Imran Khan. After the ouster of Imran Khan as Prime Minister in April 2022, the political vacuum was filled by the formation of a coalition government under the Pakistan Democratic Movement (PDM), an alliance of multiple long-time rivals such as the Pakistan Muslim League-Nawaz (PML-N) and the Pakistan People's Party (PPP), positioned itself as a necessary counterforce to Khan's PTI.

Interim government, dominated by corrupt politicians with ties to the PDM, exemplified the long-standing issues of power politics and corruption in Pakistan. After coming to power, the PDM's swift actions to eliminate corruption cases against its members only further solidified the narrative that their return to government was driven by self-preservation rather than a commitment to democratic values. Instead of ensuring fairness and neutrality, the interim government became a tool for the ruling elite to maintain control, undermining the democratic principles it was supposed to uphold. This chapter serves as a stark reminder of the challenges faced by those seeking to bring genuine reform to Pakistan's political system.

2023 Elections – The Biggest Fraud in Pakistan's History

The 2023 general elections in Pakistan marked a pivotal moment in the country's political history, as Imran Khan's Pakistan Tehreek-e-Insaf (PTI) emerged as a dominant political force, despite widespread allegations of rigging and manipulation. Khan's overwhelming support, built over decades of public service and advocacy for a "Naya Pakistan," seemed poised to secure him another term as Prime Minister. However, these elections were marred by pre-poll, poll day, and post-poll rigging, with many accusing the powerful military establishment of playing a decisive role in altering the outcome and what was meant to be a milestone for Pakistan's democracy turned into a shocking chapter of electoral fraud, manipulation, and systemic abuse, leading many to label it as the "biggest fraud in Pakistan's history."

Supporters of PTI argue that they were deprived of their rightful victory through inflated vote tallies for rival parties like PML-N and PPP. These allegations have fueled tensions and protests, with PTI calling for transparency, a thorough investigation, and a re-evaluation of the election process to restore credibility to Pakistan's democratic institutions.

Given the gravity of these accusations, such claims raise concerns about the overall integrity of the electoral process, prompting calls for electoral reforms to ensure free, fair, and transparent elections in the future.

How PTI's Victory Was Stolen

The political environment leading up to the 2023 elections was fraught with tensions. Imran Khan's ousting in 2022 through a controversial no-confidence motion had already set the stage for a polarized political landscape. Despite his removal, Khan's popularity among the masses remained high, particularly among the youth and marginalized groups, who saw him as a symbol of change and anti-corruption.

However, the military's involvement in the country's political affairs was once again a defining factor. The interim government, which was supposed to oversee the election process, was widely seen as being aligned with the military, raising concerns about its neutrality. As PTI gained momentum, opposing factions, particularly PML-N and PPP, became nervous about the prospect of Khan's return to power. This fear would soon manifest itself in a series of actions designed to derail the electoral process and prevent PTI from winning.

1. Pre-Poll Manipulations: The Establishment's Role

Months before Election Day, the pre-poll rigging had already begun, orchestrated by the military establishment under Army Chief General Qamar Javed Bajwa. Bajwa had appointed a highly controversial Chief Election Commissioner (CEC) Sikandar Sultan Raja, who was known for his close ties to the military. The CEC's actions during the election preparations made it clear that the establishment was working to undermine PTI's chances.

One of the most egregious examples of this was the irregular delimitations of electoral constituencies, which were carried out to weaken PTI's electoral strongholds. This manipulation of constituencies created an uneven playing field, giving an advantage to PTI's opponents, especially the Pakistan Muslim League-Nawaz (PML-N) and other establishment-backed parties. Every attempt was made to keep the largest and most popular political party of Imran Khan away from elections. Illegitimate delimitation and approximately 15% and in some constituencies even 20% alleged '**Ghost**' voter enrolment etc.

Prior to elections Imran Khan was sent to jail on bogus charges, members and supporters of his party were abducted, arrested, tortured and even killed. Additionally, in an attempt to cripple PTI's election campaign, the party's symbol, **the 'Bat'**, was removed, forcing PTI candidates to contest the elections as independents on a variety of different symbols. This move was designed to confuse voters and dilute PTI's brand, making it difficult for the party to mobilize its base effectively. Hundreds of various symbols were allotted to them. PTI and affiliates website was taken down so people can't find their candidates. When PTI created other alternate ways to communicate to its voters, internet was shut down throughout the country on Election Day. Even posters with fake candidates appeared on the streets to further confuse the voters.

The judiciary, under the newly appointed Chief Justice Qazi Faez Isa, also played a key role in these pre-poll manipulations. Justice Isa, known for his controversial rulings against PTI, actively sought to disqualify PTI candidates, creating legal hurdles that further weakened the party's chances. His judicial decisions appeared to align with the establishment's efforts to marginalize PTI and its leader, Imran Khan.

Despite these challenges, the public's support for PTI remained strong, with massive rallies and a vibrant social media campaign that signaled the party was still the clear favorite.

2. Poll-Day - Form 45 and Form 47 Manipulation: Altering the Results

As voting concluded on February 8, 2023, initial results from polling stations across the country showed PTI leading in a majority of constituencies at the completion of reportedly 85% of the vote count. The Form 45, which is the 'official summary of vote count' from each polling station, reflected a strong lead for PTI candidates.

However, as the results were compiled centrally, discrepancies began to emerge. The Form 47, which is the official summary of votes for each constituency, showed a stark difference from the numbers recorded on the Form 45s. The Election Commission of Pakistan (ECP), allegedly under pressure from the military establishment, altered the results on Form 47 to reduce PTI's vote count and inflate the numbers for rival parties, particularly PML-N.

In constituencies where PTI candidates were leading by thousands of votes on Form 45, they were shown to have lost after the results were compiled. This manipulation of the vote counts was widely reported, with opposition parties, analysts, and observers calling out the blatant tampering. PTI leaders and supporters were quick to highlight the discrepancies, accusing the ECP and the military of engineering the outcome to prevent Imran Khan from securing a decisive victory.

3. The Role of the Military: Media Blackout and Post-Poll Rigging

As PTI's lead became apparent by the evening of February 8, 2023, with reports indicating that the party was winning a significant number of seats, something unprecedented occurred. By 9:30 pm, TV channels across the country were abruptly taken off the air, creating a media blackout. The live reporting of election results, which had shown PTI's dominance, was halted without explanation.

Behind the scenes, the military, led by General Asim Munir, reportedly intervened to manipulate the vote counts. During the blackout, polling officials and returning officers were allegedly pressured by military personnel to alter the results. Ballot boxes were tampered with, and votes were switched in favor of PML-N and other establishment-backed candidates. The Election Commission played a complicit role by delaying the announcement of results and issuing the altered Form 47s.

When TV channels resumed their transmissions, the picture had changed dramatically. PTI's lead had evaporated, and the party was shown to have lost in key constituencies where it had been expected to win. The public outcry over this post-poll rigging was immediate, with PTI supporters accusing the military of stealing the election and subverting the democratic process.

4. Judiciary's Complicity: Undermining PTI's Legal Challenges

The judiciary, particularly under Chief Justice Qazi Faez Isa, played a critical role in legitimizing the manipulated election results. Despite widespread evidence of vote tampering and manipulation, the judiciary refused to address PTI's legal challenges. Cases filed by PTI to contest the rigged results were either dismissed outright or delayed indefinitely, preventing the party from seeking justice through the courts.

Chief Justice Isa, whose rulings had consistently favored the establishment and its allies, refused to hear PTI's petitions for recounts or investigations into the discrepancies between Form 45 and Form 47. This judicial stonewalling further entrenched the manipulated results and added to the growing sense of injustice among PTI supporters.

5. Public Turnout: A Historic Mandate for PTI

Despite the rigging and manipulation, the public's support for PTI remained overwhelming. The turnout on Election Day was historic, with millions of Pakistanis casting their votes for Imran Khan and his party. In many constituencies, even where PTI candidates were forced to run as independents due to the removal of the party's symbol, they still managed to secure significant victories, reflecting the depth of public loyalty to Khan.

The passion of PTI's supporters, particularly the youth and urban middle class, was evident throughout the election campaign. Massive rallies, extensive social media mobilization, and grassroots efforts helped galvanize a movement that transcended traditional party politics. By all accounts, PTI should have won by a landslide, but the rigging orchestrated by the military and the compromised ECP changed the outcome.

6. The Aftermath: A Compromised Victory and Continued Struggles

In the aftermath of the February 2023 elections, Imran Khan's PTI emerged as the largest party, but with a significantly reduced majority due to the rigging. The military's manipulation had ensured that PTI did not win the overwhelming mandate it was expected to receive. Instead, Khan was forced to rely on coalitions and independent candidates, weakening his government's ability to pursue the full extent of his reform agenda.

The rigging of the 2023 elections deepened the divide between the military establishment and Pakistan's civilian political leadership. PTI's supporters, who had placed their faith in the democratic process, felt betrayed by the military's interference and the judiciary's complicity. Protests erupted across the country as PTI supporters demanded accountability and transparency in the electoral process.

Imran Khan, though weakened by the rigged results, continued to press forward, vowing to fight for the rights of the Pakistani people and to expose the forces that had subverted democracy.

The Stolen Mandate – A Nation in Crisis

The final result of the 2023 elections did not reflect the clear mandate that PTI had earned from the people. Despite their decisive lead in the early hours of the election night and a high voter turnout, PTI was deprived of its victory. The stolen mandate left the people of Pakistan disillusioned and enraged, with many questioning the fairness and transparency of the entire electoral process.

Imran Khan, who had steadfastly campaigned on the promise of a Naya Pakistan (New Pakistan), rejected the results, calling the election a "stolen election" and accusing the establishment of thwarting the will of the people. His supporters, who had believed in him as the voice of the oppressed, now found themselves at odds with a system that appeared to be designed to keep the political elite in power.

The manipulation of the election results, along with the military's decisive role, further deepened the divide between the establishment and the people of Pakistan. The post-poll rigging created an atmosphere of mistrust and suspicion, not just against the ruling parties but also against the military, which many believed had undermined the democratic process to maintain its own influence.

International Observations and Media Censorship

International observers, who had been monitoring the elections, also raised concerns about the electoral integrity. Many international bodies and foreign governments questioned the legitimacy of the 2023 elections, with some expressing concerns over the transparency of the vote count and the role of the military in the process. However, the international response was muted, with some countries opting to turn a blind eye to the crisis, likely due to geopolitical considerations.

At the same time, media censorship became rampant, as many news outlets and journalists who were covering the election fraud were silenced or intimidated. Independent media platforms sympathetic to PTI were particularly targeted, and their reports about election malpractices were suppressed. This created a vacuum of information, with the official narrative, heavily controlled by the establishment, becoming the only version of events available to the public.

Conclusion – A Betrayal of Democracy

The 2023 elections will forever be remembered as a betrayal of democracy in Pakistan. What should have been a fair and transparent process to decide the future of the country turned into a dark chapter of manipulation and blatant fraud. The high voter turnout, the overwhelming support for PTI, and the apparent victory of Khan's party were all overshadowed by post-poll rigging and the military's involvement in altering the outcome of the election.

The stolen mandate and the way the election results were tweaked left the people of Pakistan with a deep sense of betrayal. What was meant to be a peaceful transition of power became a bitter reminder of how entrenched political forces, military influence, and systemic corruption could undermine the will of the people.

As Pakistan continues to grapple with its democratic crisis, the 2023 elections stand as a testament to how easily the electoral process can be manipulated. With growing unrest among the public and ongoing protests, the true verdict of the people of Pakistan remains unclear, and it is uncertain when they will have the opportunity to reclaim their voice. The 2023 election fraud will remain a scar on Pakistan's political history, and the battle for democracy continues.

The Unwavering Support for Imran Khan Post-2023 Fraudulent Election

The 2023 general election in Pakistan marked a significant turning point in the nation's political landscape. Allegations of widespread fraud, manipulation, and interference marred the process, leading to protests and unrest across the country. At the heart of this movement stood Imran Khan, the former Prime Minister and leader of the Pakistan Tehreek-e-Insaf (PTI), who claimed that the election was stolen from him and his party. Despite an intense crackdown by the government and military authorities, Khan's popularity surged, supported by an unrelenting wave of social media activism that transcended traditional media restrictions.

A Rigged Election and the Rise of Dissent

The 2023 election was meant to be a decisive contest between PTI and the traditional political powerhouses—Pakistan Muslim League-Nawaz (PML-N) and Pakistan People's Party (PPP). However, as results started trickling in, it became clear that the election was far from fair. Reports of ballot stuffing, voter suppression, and intimidation by local authorities surfaced.

Many believed that the powerful military establishment, along with the political elite, had worked together to ensure PTI's defeat. Imran Khan's supporters quickly labeled it a "fraud election."

Khan's own arrest and disqualification from running further exacerbated tensions. The government, in conjunction with the military, launched an aggressive campaign to curb any mention of Imran Khan's name across regulated media. TV channels, newspapers, and radio stations were barred from covering him or showing his image. This blackout extended to government-controlled online platforms, effectively erasing Khan from the public's immediate access through traditional means.

But the move backfired in unprecedented ways. Far from quelling dissent, these draconian measures sparked a digital revolution that the government and military failed to foresee or control.

The Power of Social Media: A New Battlefield

While mainstream media had been largely silenced or coerced, social media platforms became the lifeline for Imran Khan's message. PTI's well-established digital presence, cultivated during Khan's years in power, now became the party's strongest weapon. Through platforms like Twitter, Facebook, YouTube, TikTok, and WhatsApp, PTI supporters, famously known as the "PTI Tigers," kept the movement alive.

Even as the government attempted to restrict access to these platforms, PTI's online presence only grew. Khan's supporters employed virtual private networks (VPNs) to bypass government censorship, posting videos of protests, speeches, and evidence of government corruption. Within minutes of any government narrative or propaganda hitting the airwaves, PTI's social media activists would dismantle it, offering counter-narratives backed by videos, photos, and real-time commentary. These "Tigers" quickly debunked false claims, forcing the government into a state of helplessness.

A Silent Defeat for the so called Establishment

Despite its control over regulated media and its efforts to squash dissent through censorship and repression, the government found itself unable to match PTI's rapid and agile social media machine. Every time a new story was concocted to undermine Khan's credibility or paint him as a destabilizing force, PTI's social media activists countered it with vigor. For every government speech trying to demonize Khan, there were thousands of posts, tweets, and videos defending him and exposing what PTI saw as the hypocrisy of the political elite.

The speed and reach of social media overwhelmed the government's traditional media machinery. With users from every corner of Pakistan and across the global diaspora, Khan's popularity spread even in areas once considered strongholds of his political rivals. In cities like Lahore and Multan—historically aligned with PML-N and PPP—pro-Khan sentiment grew, particularly among younger voters. This was largely because of social media's ability to bypass the government's restrictions and deliver uncensored information directly to the people.

This newfound political dynamism was particularly stark in urban centers but also trickled into rural areas, where cell phone penetration had increased dramatically in recent years. PTI's supporters shared content across class lines, making Khan's voice omnipresent in a media landscape that sought to erase him.

The Collapse of the Government's Narrative

The military and the government, for all their power and control, found themselves at a loss. The traditional method of controlling the public narrative—through TV anchors, columnists, and state-run media channels—was no longer enough. With each new press conference or public statement, government officials attempted to blame Khan and PTI for unrest, lawlessness, and economic instability. But these accusations fell flat as PTI's digital army responded almost instantaneously, mobilizing in defense of their leader.

The government's counter-narratives, designed to portray Khan as a destabilizing figure or a foreign agent, were quickly dismantled by social media posts with counter-evidence or logical arguments. Photos of protests, hashtags, and viral memes flooded the internet, reinforcing Khan's image as a victim of state oppression rather than a perpetrator of chaos. Every misstep by the government was recorded, circulated, and scrutinized online, feeding into the growing disillusionment with the political establishment.

Even outside of Pakistan, the diaspora played a crucial role in shaping the narrative. PTI supporters abroad organized rallies and campaigns, amplifying Khan's cause on global platforms. This international dimension further complicated the government's attempts to control the narrative, as it was now fighting on multiple fronts.

A Growing Challenge in Traditional Strongholds

What was even more remarkable was the way Khan's message resonated in areas previously dominated by PML-N and PPP. Cities like Lahore, Gujranwala, Sialkot, and Nawabshah—long considered bastions of these parties—saw an increase in pro-PTI sentiments, with growing disillusionment toward the entrenched leadership. Videos of local rallies supporting Khan surfaced on social media, surprising political analysts who had long viewed these regions as impenetrable for PTI.

This shift highlighted a broader transformation in Pakistan's political landscape. No longer could political elites rely on their traditional voter bases. The advent of social media, coupled with Imran Khan's relentless focus on corruption, justice, and transparency, had created a wave of political consciousness that transcended party lines.

The Government's Silence: A Sign of Defeat

Faced with this growing, uncontrollable mass movement, the government and military were left numb. They attempted to resort to authoritarian tactics—arrests, shutdowns, and censorship—but the genie was already out of the bottle. With each new repressive measure, Khan's popularity only seemed to grow, as people rallied around him, seeing him as a symbol of resistance against an outdated and unjust system.

Unable to build a coherent narrative or combat PTI's social media juggernaut, the government's silence in the face of widespread dissent spoke volumes. The military, traditionally a key player in Pakistani politics, also found itself outmatched in the digital arena. Its reputation, once carefully controlled, took a hit as PTI's social media activists exposed various missteps and criticized their role in the political manipulation.

Conclusion: A New Political Era

The 2023 election and its aftermath marked a profound shift in Pakistani politics. Imran Khan's enduring popularity, driven by an empowered and tech-savvy social media base, fundamentally changed the way political narratives are constructed and contested in Pakistan. Despite the military and government's best efforts to suppress his voice and erase him from the public sphere, Khan emerged stronger than ever. His supporters, leveraging the power of social media, turned censorship and repression into fuel for their movement.

In this new digital era, the people—not the state—control the narrative. And for the political elite in Pakistan, this new reality presents a challenge that will not be easily overcome.

Why Imran Khan Was Removed?

Imran Khan's rise to power and the subsequent economic growth Pakistan experienced under his leadership became a significant challenge for not only his political opponents but also powerful international forces. His focus on self-reliance, reducing dependency on foreign aid, and creating an economically independent Pakistan disrupted the geopolitical status quo. This chapter will explore the reasons behind why Khan's government was ousted, with a focus on how Pakistan's success may have threatened the interests of powerful international establishments.

1. Challenging the Global Status Quo

Under Imran Khan, Pakistan began to take steps toward self-sufficiency, reducing its reliance on international financial institutions and foreign aid. Khan's government emphasized economic independence, bolstered by growing exports, increased foreign reserves, and reforms in key sectors such as agriculture and technology. His success in managing the economy during the global COVID-19 crisis, when many other nations struggled, demonstrated the potential of Pakistan to emerge as a more resilient and self-reliant state.

This growing strength posed a challenge to the international establishment, particularly the global financial order dominated by institutions like the International Monetary Fund (IMF) and the World Bank. Khan's government negotiated tough terms with the IMF but was also critical of the long-standing reliance on such financial institutions, which many developing countries, including Pakistan, saw as perpetuating debt traps rather than fostering sustainable growth.

Additionally, Khan's foreign policy, which aimed to diversify Pakistan's alliances, building closer ties with China and Russia, may have been viewed as a threat by Western powers. His stance on various international issues, including his criticism of U.S. foreign policy and calls for a more just and equitable world order, positioned him as a leader willing to challenge global powers. Such moves likely raised concerns among international elites who benefit from maintaining the existing global economic and political systems.

2. Economic Success: A Threat to Global Interests?

One of the major reasons behind the effort to stop Imran Khan's government could be Pakistan's rising economic success under his leadership. Pakistan's export growth, particularly in textiles and information technology, and the focus on local industries were key drivers of the economy. Khan's policies to incentivize local businesses and industries made Pakistan less dependent on foreign goods and investment, creating a more self-sufficient economy.

At the same time, Khan's emphasis on strengthening regional trade and economic ties, particularly with China through the China-Pakistan Economic Corridor (CPEC), created new avenues for growth outside the influence of Western-controlled markets. This strategic alignment with non-Western powers may have been perceived as a move that could reduce Pakistan's economic dependency on Western countries and financial institutions.

For certain global players, a strong and economically independent Pakistan under Khan's leadership might have been seen as an obstacle to maintaining geopolitical control in South Asia. Pakistan's growing ties with China, coupled with Khan's independent foreign policy, may have fueled fears that Pakistan would drift further away from Western influence, limiting their leverage over the region's economic and political dynamics.

3. Khan's Anti-Corruption Crusade: Disrupting Local and International Power Structures

One of Imran Khan's signature policies was his relentless fight against corruption. This crusade targeted not only domestic political elites but also international networks that benefit from corrupt practices in developing countries. By cracking down on financial malpractices and promoting transparency, Khan's government disrupted powerful vested interests within Pakistan, particularly the entrenched political dynasties that had long dominated the country's politics and economy.

Khan's anti-corruption drive also sent shockwaves internationally. His stance on money laundering and efforts to bring back illicit wealth stashed abroad created friction with global actors who benefit from such financial flows. His government actively sought to recover assets held by corrupt politicians in foreign banks, a move that directly challenged the status quo of international financial systems that often protect illicit capital.

This anti-corruption drive further distanced Khan from the global elite, who thrive on maintaining financial opacity in developing nations. Khan's efforts to hold domestic and international actors accountable for corruption may have placed him at odds with both local oligarchs and international financial networks, making him a target for removal.

4. Geopolitical Realignment and Foreign Policy Independence

Khan's foreign policy during his tenure focused on recalibrating Pakistan's relations with the world, reducing reliance on Western powers, and fostering stronger ties with regional powers like China, Russia, Turkey, and Malaysia. His decision to maintain a neutral stance in international conflicts, such as the U.S.-China rivalry and the Russia-Ukraine conflict, may have angered traditional allies, particularly in the West, who saw Pakistan as a key player in their geopolitical strategies in South Asia.

Khan's refusal to allow Pakistan to be used as a pawn in global conflicts, along with his criticism of U.S. military interventions in the region, notably Afghanistan, created tensions with Western powers. His government's refusal to grant the U.S. military bases in Pakistan post-Afghanistan withdrawal was a major point of contention.

Furthermore, Khan's vocal stance on issues like Islamophobia and the rights of Muslims in the global arena positioned him as a leader willing to stand up against Western double standards. His speeches at the United Nations and other international forums brought attention to these issues, which may have alienated powerful Western interests.

This foreign policy independence made Khan a liability for those who preferred a more pliant Pakistani leadership that would align with their global strategies. His efforts to foster regional cooperation outside Western influence, along with his resistance to being drawn into great power conflicts, may have contributed to efforts to undermine his government.

5. Internal Political Challenges and the Role of the Powerful Military

In addition to external forces, internal political dynamics played a key role in Khan's ouster. His government faced opposition from traditional political elites, particularly the Pakistan Muslim League-Nawaz (PML-N) and Pakistan Peoples Party (PPP), who had been sidelined by Khan's rise. These parties, backed by powerful interest groups within Pakistan's establishment, had a vested interest in bringing down Khan's government to regain control of the political system.

Khan's often tense relationship with the military establishment, particularly after the appointment of key military positions, may have also contributed to his ouster. While initially aligned with the establishment, tensions grew over policy disagreements and Khan's increasing assertiveness in decision-making. The political instability that followed created an opening for his opponents to mobilize and eventually remove him from power through a parliamentary no-confidence vote.

6. Conclusion: A Threat to the Global and Local Power Structures

Imran Khan's tenure as Prime Minister of Pakistan was characterized by a vision of economic independence, anti-corruption, and foreign policy autonomy. These policies, which sought to make Pakistan a more self-sufficient and sovereign nation, challenged both domestic power elites and international establishments that have long benefited from maintaining Pakistan's dependency.

Khan's focus on economic growth, transparency, and reducing foreign influence may have made him a target for those who stood to lose from a more independent and prosperous Pakistan. His removal from power was not just the result of internal political opposition but also the culmination of external pressures and interests threatened by Pakistan's success under his leadership.

While Khan's government may have been ousted, his legacy remains influential, as his supporters continue to view him as a leader who dared to challenge the forces that have historically held Pakistan back from reaching its full potential.

India and the U.S. Involvement in Pakistan's Power Game

Pakistan's internal politics have long been influenced by a combination of domestic factors and external pressures. Among the most significant foreign players with vested interests in Pakistan's power dynamics are its neighbor, India, and the United States. Both nations have historically maintained a complex and strategic relationship with Pakistan, often shaped by broader geopolitical concerns in South Asia, including the balance of power, regional security, and economic interests. This chapter delves into the roles India and the U.S. have played in Pakistan's political landscape, with a particular focus on their involvement during Imran Khan's tenure as Prime Minister and his eventual ousting.

1. U.S. Involvement: Strategic Interests and Shifting Alliances

a. Pakistan's Geopolitical Role

Pakistan has traditionally been a key ally of the U.S. due to its strategic location, particularly in relation to Afghanistan, China, and India. For decades, U.S.-Pakistan relations were underpinned by military cooperation, economic aid, and Pakistan's role in counterterrorism operations, especially in the context of the U.S.-led war on terror. However, during Imran Khan's time in power, the dynamics of this relationship began to shift.

Khan's government sought to redefine Pakistan's foreign policy, moving towards greater independence and lessening the country's reliance on the West, especially the U.S. This shift was evident in several of Khan's decisions, such as his refusal to allow the U.S. military to use Pakistani bases for operations in Afghanistan following the U.S. withdrawal. Khan's increasing tilt towards China and Russia, as well as his critical stance on U.S. military interventions, strained relations with Washington.

b. The Russia-Ukraine Conflict and Khan's Neutrality

One of the key turning points in the relationship between Imran Khan's government and the U.S. came with the onset of the Russia-Ukraine conflict in early 2022. While the U.S. and its Western allies were rallying global support for sanctions against Russia, Khan chose a neutral stance. In fact, he made a high-profile visit to Moscow and met with President Vladimir Putin just as the Ukraine crisis was unfolding, a move that angered the U.S. and its European partners. This visit was perceived as Khan positioning Pakistan as an independent actor on the global stage, unwilling to be drawn into Cold War-style alliances.

For Washington, Khan's neutrality and growing ties with Russia and China were seen as problematic, given the broader geopolitical struggle between the U.S. and these powers. The U.S. has long sought to limit Russia's influence in the region and viewed Khan's government as drifting away from the West's strategic goals. Khan's stance was in stark contrast to previous Pakistani governments, which had been more aligned with U.S. foreign policy interests.

c. The "Regime Change" Narrative

Imran Khan, following his ousting through a no-confidence vote in April 2022, repeatedly claimed that his removal from power was orchestrated by the U.S. in collaboration with local actors in Pakistan. He pointed to a diplomatic cable allegedly sent by Pakistan's then-ambassador to Washington, which he claimed contained threats from a U.S. official demanding Khan's removal due to his foreign policy decisions, particularly regarding neutrality in the Russia-Ukraine war.

While the U.S. government has consistently denied involvement in Khan's ouster, the narrative of foreign interference resonated with many of Khan's supporters. They believed that the U.S. had a vested interest in removing a leader who was moving Pakistan away from its traditional alignment with Western powers and forging closer ties with Russia and China.

2. India's Involvement: Regional Rivalry and Internal Destabilization

a. India-Pakistan Rivalry

India's involvement in Pakistan's power game is primarily driven by the historical and deeply entrenched rivalry between the two nations. Since partition in 1947, India and Pakistan have fought several wars and engaged in numerous skirmishes, particularly over the disputed region of Kashmir. For India, Pakistan's internal stability—or lack thereof—has direct implications for regional security and its own geopolitical standing.

Imran Khan's tenure saw a further deterioration in India-Pakistan relations, particularly after the Pulwama attack in February 2019 and the subsequent Balakot airstrike. Tensions between the two nuclear-armed neighbors reached a peak, with Khan playing a central role in the diplomatic and military responses. He strongly criticized India's actions in Kashmir, especially after the Indian government revoked the special status of Jammu and Kashmir in August 2019, which led to increased international attention on the issue. Khan's vocal support for the Kashmiri people and his calls for global intervention angered India, which viewed his leadership as a threat to its regional dominance.

b. India's Alleged Destabilization Efforts

While direct Indian involvement in Pakistan's internal politics is difficult to prove, there have long been allegations that India seeks to destabilize Pakistan by supporting separatist movements and insurgencies, particularly in regions like Balochistan. Pakistan's security agencies have frequently accused Indian intelligence of funding and arming militant groups to weaken Pakistan from within. During Khan's time in power, these accusations continued, with Islamabad claiming that India was attempting to foment unrest in Pakistan to distract from its own internal issues and to weaken Pakistan's growing regional influence.

Khan's efforts to strengthen Pakistan's military capabilities, improve its economy, and foster closer ties with China through the China-Pakistan Economic Corridor (CPEC) were seen by India as a direct challenge to its own strategic interests in the region. India's opposition to CPEC, which passes through the disputed territory of Gilgit-Baltistan, was well-known, and New Delhi may have viewed Khan's leadership as an obstacle to its efforts to counter China's influence in South Asia.

c. The Afghanistan Factor

Another critical aspect of India's involvement in Pakistan's internal affairs relates to Afghanistan. For years, India has cultivated a strong relationship with successive Afghan governments, while Pakistan has had a more complicated and sometimes adversarial relationship with Kabul, particularly with regard to the Taliban. Khan's government played a significant role in facilitating the U.S.-Taliban peace talks and the eventual withdrawal of U.S. troops from Afghanistan. This development, which strengthened the Taliban's position in Afghanistan, was viewed with concern by India, as it reduced New Delhi's influence in Kabul and bolstered Pakistan's strategic depth in the region.

Some analysts suggest that India, unhappy with the Taliban's resurgence and Pakistan's role in it, may have sought to undermine Khan's government, which was seen as too close to the Taliban and unwilling to accommodate India's interests in the post-U.S. Afghanistan landscape. While there is no concrete evidence of direct Indian involvement in Khan's ouster, the broader regional rivalry between the two nations certainly played a role in shaping the political landscape during his tenure.

3. Conclusion: A Complex Power Game

The involvement of both the U.S. and India in Pakistan's internal power game reflects the complex interplay of domestic and international factors that have long shaped the country's political trajectory. For the U.S., Khan's government represented a challenge to its strategic interests in South Asia, particularly as Pakistan moved closer to China and Russia. For India, Khan's leadership was seen as a threat to its regional dominance, particularly in light of his vocal support for Kashmir and his government's role in Afghanistan.

While Imran Khan's removal from power was ultimately the result of domestic political maneuvering, it is clear that external pressures, particularly from the U.S. and India, played a role in shaping the broader context in which his government operated. Khan's efforts to steer Pakistan towards greater independence, both economically and in foreign policy, likely contributed to the desire of powerful international actors to see him removed from office.

Pakistan's Resources Under Siege by Corrupt Military and Political Pundits

Pakistan, a land brimming with natural wealth and untapped potential, finds itself crippled by a persistent and deep-rooted problem: the control of its resources by corrupt military generals and political elites. Over the years, these ruling factions, often acting as proxies for foreign powers, have turned Pakistan's vast wealth into personal fortunes, while the country's development remains stunted. With over 6 trillion dollars' worth of resources at stake, including the highly coveted Reko-Diq mineral reserves, Pakistan's riches have been systematically exploited by the very leaders entrusted to protect and harness them.

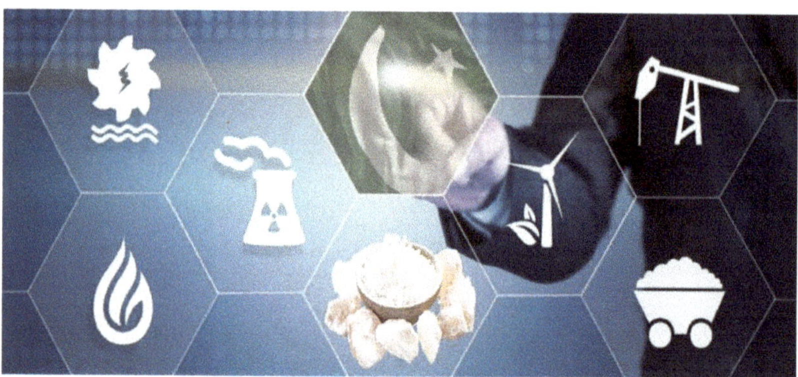

A Wealth of Untapped Resources

Pakistan is home to some of the world's most valuable natural resources. The country's land offers vast reserves of precious metals, coal, natural gas, and fertile agricultural plains. The mineral-rich Balochistan province alone holds untold wealth, including the Reko Diq copper-gold mine, which is estimated to hold $1 trillion worth of minerals. The Thar coalfields possess one of the largest coal reserves in the world, capable of powering the country's energy needs for decades. These resources, if managed properly, could transform Pakistan into a major economic powerhouse.

Yet, despite these immense opportunities, Pakistan's population has seen little benefit from this wealth. Decades of mismanagement, corruption, and foreign interference have left the country dependent on loans from international institutions, while a small elite continues to extract personal wealth from the nation's treasures. This tragic paradox stems from the capture of Pakistan's resources by a corrupt nexus of military and political leaders, many of whom are in the pockets of foreign powers seeking to profit from Pakistan's wealth.

Corrupt Generals and Politicians: Proxies for Foreign Powers

At the heart of Pakistan's resource exploitation is the unholy alliance between corrupt military generals and politicians. Over time, these elites have not only gained control over domestic resources but have also acted as brokers for foreign interests. Driven by greed, they have mortgaged Pakistan's sovereignty and allowed foreign powers to dictate terms on the country's most valuable assets.

Military generals, whose role was historically meant to defend the nation, have long expanded their influence into economic and political spheres. The military's business empire spans real estate, industrial ventures, and infrastructure development, granting it enormous influence over the country's economic decisions. While the military has justified this involvement as serving the nation's interest, it has become clear that many of these ventures benefit a select few at the top rather than the country as a whole.

Political dynasties such as the Sharifs, Bhuttos and Zardaris have similarly treated Pakistan's resources as their personal inheritance. These families have ruled in an alternating pattern, leaving a trail of corruption, embezzlement, and mismanagement. Whether it is through securing lucrative contracts, manipulating the banking system, or selling national assets to foreign companies, these political leaders have actively sought to enrich themselves at the cost of national progress.

Behind this corruption lies the influence of foreign powers— countries and corporations that eye Pakistan's wealth, particularly its mineral resources, with great interest. In exchange for personal wealth and political favor, Pakistan's corrupt elite has granted foreign firms access to the nation's resources at rock-bottom prices, selling off the country's future to line their own pockets.

The Case of Reko Diq: A Billion-Dollar Scandal

The Reko Diq mine in Balochistan represents one of the most egregious examples of this corruption. Reko Diq, with its massive deposits of copper and gold, is considered one of the largest untapped resources of its kind in the world, with an estimated value of over $1 trillion. The potential for Reko Diq to generate jobs, boost the local economy, and provide the country with significant revenue is immense. However, instead of being used for national development, Reko Diq has become a battleground for foreign interests, backed by corrupt local officials.

In 2011, the Pakistani government canceled the license of the foreign mining companies operating at Reko Diq, leading to a prolonged legal battle that culminated in an international arbitration case. Pakistan was slapped with a massive $6 billion fine by the International Centre for Settlement of Investment Disputes (ICSID), an outcome that was a direct result of the shady dealings between local political elites and foreign corporations. The deal-making process had been riddled with corruption, lack of transparency, and disregard for national interest.

While Reko Diq was meant to be a lifeline for Balochistan's impoverished communities, the profits were funneled to foreign companies and local elites, leaving the region to languish in poverty. The corrupt officials who facilitated these deals enriched themselves at the expense of the nation, while foreign powers exploited the resources that should have belonged to the people of Pakistan.

Foreign Powers Eyeing Pakistan's Wealth

Pakistan's strategic location and abundant natural resources have made it a target for global powers seeking to secure access to raw materials and strategic footholds. Countries like China, the United States, and Gulf states have all sought to gain influence in Pakistan, often through lucrative deals with the military and political leadership.

The China-Pakistan Economic Corridor (CPEC), while touted as a game-changing infrastructure project, has raised concerns about how much of Pakistan's resources are being handed over to foreign control. Although CPEC promises much-needed investment in roads, energy, and trade routes, it has also provided China with significant leverage over Pakistan's economy. Chinese companies are securing access to key industries, including mining and energy, often through deals negotiated behind closed doors with Pakistan's elite.

In many cases, these deals come with strings attached—high-interest loans, control over strategic resources, and long-term obligations that tie Pakistan's future to foreign interests. The corrupt generals and politicians, blinded by short-term gains, have been all too willing to sacrifice Pakistan's sovereignty for personal enrichment. This has left the country trapped in a cycle of dependence, with its most valuable assets effectively under foreign control.

A Growing Crisis: The Helplessness of the Nation

While Pakistan's military generals and political elites continue to enrich themselves through their control of national resources, the country's people suffer the consequences. The economic inequality, lack of access to basic services, and chronic underdevelopment are all symptoms of this exploitative system. As foreign powers and corrupt elites tighten their grip on Pakistan's wealth, the majority of the population is left to contend with high inflation, unemployment, and a failing infrastructure.

This concentration of power has also led to a growing sense of helplessness within Pakistan. The state's institutions have been hollowed out by corruption, leaving little room for accountability. Attempts to challenge this status quo—whether through protests, legal action, or political opposition—are quickly quashed by the military and political elite, who use their control over the media, judiciary, and security forces to maintain their grip on power.

Social Media and Popular Resistance

Despite these challenges, a new wave of resistance is beginning to form. Social media has emerged as a powerful tool for exposing corruption and rallying public support against the entrenched elite. Platforms like Twitter, Facebook, and YouTube have allowed ordinary Pakistanis to bypass state-controlled media and share information about the exploitation of the country's resources.

Movements like Pakistan Tehreek-e-Insaf (PTI), led by Imran Khan, have capitalized on this digital revolution, using social media to galvanize public opinion against the corrupt establishment. Even with attempts by the government and military to censor and suppress voices calling for change, the message of accountability and reform continues to spread across the country.

The people of Pakistan, particularly its youth, are increasingly demanding transparency and an end to the corrupt practices that have plagued the nation for decades. The growing awareness of how deeply Pakistan's resources have been sold off to foreign interests has ignited a sense of urgency to reclaim the nation's sovereignty and wealth.

Conclusion: The Fight for Pakistan's Future

Pakistan's over 6 trillion dollars' worth of resources—including Reko Diq—should be a source of national pride and development. Instead, these assets have been hijacked by corrupt generals and political elites, many of whom act as proxies for foreign powers with vested interests in keeping Pakistan weak and dependent.

The challenge for Pakistan is to wrest control of its resources from the grip of these corrupt forces. This will require a political and economic overhaul, led by movements dedicated to transparency, accountability, and national sovereignty. The people of Pakistan, through grassroots activism and social media, are already beginning to fight back against this system of exploitation.

The road to reclaiming Pakistan's wealth will be long and difficult, but with a renewed sense of purpose and a growing awareness of the country's potential, there is hope that Pakistan can one day break free from the siege of corruption and foreign control, and finally harness its resources for the benefit of all its citizens.

Economic Hit Man: Pakistan as a Clear Example

The term Economic Hit Man (EHM), popularized by John Perkins in his book Confessions of an Economic Hit Man, refers to individuals who manipulate the economies of developing nations through debt, creating dependency on powerful financial institutions like the IMF or World Bank. They essentially push nations into a debt trap, forcing them to align their policies with the interests of foreign powers and multinational corporations at the expense of their own sovereignty.

Pakistan stands as a clear example of this phenomenon. Over the years, the country has fallen into a cycle of borrowing, debt restructuring, and economic crises, making it heavily reliant on external financial bodies for survival. This dependency has led to the erosion of its economic autonomy, with foreign powers dictating key policy decisions that often harm local industries, increase inflation, and exacerbate poverty.

Some ways Pakistan mirrors the Economic Hit Man model include:

1. Mounting Debt:

Pakistan's national debt has soared due to repeated loans from the IMF and other international creditors. Each loan comes with stringent conditions that require economic reforms—often in the form of austerity measures. These measures cut public spending, impacting health, education, and infrastructure, while foreign corporations profit from exploitative business terms.

2. Policy Manipulation:

The IMF and World Bank frequently impose policies that undermine Pakistan's ability to implement an independent economic strategy. The conditions attached to their loans have often required devaluation of the currency, removal of subsidies, and increased taxes, disproportionately affecting the middle and lower classes. These conditions primarily benefit multinational corporations and foreign investors while leaving Pakistan in a constant state of economic instability.

3. Resource Exploitation:

Like many developing countries, Pakistan's rich natural resources, such as Reko-Diq's copper and gold reserves, have attracted the attention of foreign powers and corporations. The deals made often involve terms that deprive Pakistan of its fair share of profits, leaving the country with minimal benefits while foreign entities profit immensely. These agreements are typically signed under financial duress, often when Pakistan is desperate for funds to service its debt, locking the nation into exploitative arrangements.

4. Political Control through Economic Pressure:

Pakistan's economic vulnerability has allowed foreign nations to exert political influence. The dependency on loans gives creditors the leverage to pressure Pakistan into aligning its foreign and domestic policies with their interests, even when these policies are against Pakistan's long-term development goals or sovereignty.

Conclusion:

Pakistan's experience with economic dependency and external manipulation is a textbook case of how Economic Hit Man tactics can erode a nation's sovereignty. The cycle of debt and dependency traps the country in a position where it cannot make independent economic decisions, perpetuating poverty and inequality. This has made Pakistan's economic recovery difficult, while allowing foreign powers to maintain significant influence over its political and economic affairs. The only path out of this vicious cycle is for Pakistan to regain control over its resources, negotiate fairer deals, and pursue policies that benefit its people rather than catering to the interests of international creditors.

Awakening of Public Consciousness and Unprecedented Support for Khan

The political landscape of Pakistan has been marked by a history of power struggles between entrenched political dynasties, military interventions, and external influences. However, the rise of Imran Khan as a transformative leader has brought about an unprecedented shift in the nation's public consciousness. With an overwhelming majority of the population—estimated at nearly 95%—standing behind him at the peak of his popularity, Khan has become more than just a political figure. He has emerged as a symbol of hope, resistance, and national pride for millions of Pakistanis.

This mass mobilization and near-universal support for a single leader is unparalleled in the country's history, making it a pivotal moment in Pakistan's journey toward a more engaged, politically aware, and empowered citizenry. This chapter explores the factors that led to this awakening of public consciousness, the role Imran Khan played in this transformation, and the implications for the future of Pakistan.

1. Historical Context: A Country Disillusioned with the Status Quo

Before Imran Khan's meteoric rise to political power, Pakistan's political landscape was dominated by a sense of cynicism and disillusionment. Decades of rule by two major political dynasties—the Pakistan Peoples Party (PPP) and the Pakistan Muslim League-Nawaz (PML-N)—had left many Pakistanis feeling disempowered and excluded from the political process. Corruption scandals, economic mismanagement, and the military's recurring interventions in politics had further eroded public trust in the state's ability to deliver justice, prosperity, or true democracy.

For much of its history, Pakistan's political narrative was defined by patronage networks, elitism, and power politics, where the needs of the ordinary citizen often took a back seat to the interests of the powerful few. This environment of disenfranchisement and frustration created fertile ground for the emergence of a leader who could tap into the latent desire for change.

Imran Khan, a former cricket hero and philanthropist, stepped into this vacuum with a message that resonated deeply with the masses. He spoke of justice, anti-corruption, and self-reliance, promising to break the cycle of dynastic politics and deliver a "New Pakistan" that would be accountable, transparent, and focused on the needs of the people. His party, Pakistan Tehreek-e-Insaf (PTI), positioned itself as the voice of the voiceless, offering an alternative to the entrenched elites that had long controlled the political system.

2. The Role of Imran Khan: A Leader for the People

Imran Khan's appeal lies not only in his promises of reform but also in his unique ability to connect with the aspirations of ordinary Pakistanis. Unlike the leaders of the traditional political parties, Khan is perceived as a man of integrity, untainted by corruption scandals, and someone who genuinely wants to improve the lives of the people. His rise was fueled by his personal story of resilience—from a cricketing legend who led Pakistan to victory in the 1992 World Cup to a philanthropist who built the Shaukat Khanum Cancer Hospital—and his vision of a self-sufficient and proud Pakistan.

Khan's message of an independent foreign policy—one free from the dictates of foreign powers, particularly the United States—resonated with a public that had long felt its country was being used as a pawn in global geopolitical games. His famous declaration of "Absolutely Not" in response to U.S. requests for bases in Pakistan symbolized his commitment to Pakistan's sovereignty and struck a chord with a population that was tired of external interference in their nation's affairs.

Moreover, Khan's emphasis on justice (insaf) and the establishment of a welfare state, inspired by Islamic principles, appealed to a wide cross-section of the population. His vision of a government that would be accountable to the people, where the rich and powerful would be held to the same standards as the ordinary citizen, created a sense of hope and empowerment that had not been seen in decades.

3. The Youth Factor: A Generation of Change-Makers

A critical element in the unprecedented support for Imran Khan has been the youth of Pakistan, who make up a significant portion of the country's population. This younger generation, disillusioned with the corrupt political elites and the lack of opportunities, found in Khan a leader who spoke their language and understood their frustrations. He gave them a sense of purpose and agency, encouraging them to become active participants in shaping their country's future.

Khan's campaign relied heavily on social media and grassroots organizing, which allowed him to mobilize the youth in ways that traditional political parties had never managed. His rallies, often resembling mass movements, were filled with young people from all walks of life—urban and rural, educated and working-class—who saw in Khan the promise of a better, more just Pakistan.

This youth-driven movement was not just about political support but a larger cultural shift in the way Pakistanis viewed their role in society. The youth were no longer passive observers of a corrupt system; they were now active change-makers, demanding transparency, accountability, and progress. This shift in public consciousness has been one of the most significant outcomes of Khan's rise, as it signaled the awakening of a new, politically engaged generation.

4. A Unifying Force: From Urban Centers to Rural Heartlands

Imran Khan's support cuts across Pakistan's diverse social, ethnic, and geographical divides, making his popularity truly unprecedented. Traditionally, Pakistani politics has been deeply fragmented, with different regions and ethnic groups aligning with specific political parties. However, Khan's message of national unity and his focus on addressing economic inequality, corruption, and justice transcended these divides, bringing together a broad coalition of Pakistanis under one banner.

From the bustling urban centers of Karachi, Lahore, and Islamabad to the rural heartlands of Punjab, Khyber Pakhtunkhwa, and Sindh, Khan's supporters come from all segments of society. His ability to connect with people across these divides has made him a unifying force, something that Pakistan had not seen in decades.

This unity is particularly striking given Pakistan's historical divisions along ethnic, religious, and class lines. Khan's narrative of a "Naya Pakistan" (New Pakistan) tapped into a shared desire for a better future, where justice would be served to all citizens regardless of their background. This sense of collective hope has been one of the most powerful driving forces behind his unprecedented support.

5. Challenges and Criticisms: A Polarized Nation

While Khan's support is vast and passionate, it has also been met with resistance from the traditional political establishment and sections of the media. Critics argue that his tenure as Prime Minister saw mixed results in governance, with economic challenges and political instability marking his time in office. They also accuse him of being authoritarian and of undermining democratic institutions in his quest to consolidate power.

Additionally, Khan's rise has polarized the nation, with his supporters viewing him as a messianic figure who can do no wrong, while his detractors see him as a populist who has failed to deliver on many of his promises. This polarization has led to a deeply divided political climate, where compromise and consensus-building have become increasingly difficult.

However, despite these criticisms, Khan's supporters remain fiercely loyal, seeing him as the only leader capable of breaking the cycle of corruption and foreign dependency that has plagued Pakistan for decades.

Imran Khan's phrase "Absolutely Not" became one of the most iconic and popular expressions of his tenure as Prime Minister of Pakistan. It gained widespread attention in 2021 during an interview when Khan was asked whether Pakistan would allow the U.S. to use Pakistani military bases for operations in Afghanistan following the withdrawal of U.S. troops from the region.

Context of "Absolutely Not"

At the time, the U.S. was seeking bases in the region to continue its counterterrorism operations after withdrawing from Afghanistan. Speculations arose that the U.S. might ask Pakistan for access to its airbases, as had been the case in the past during the War on Terror. In response to a question about whether Pakistan would allow the U.S. to use its territory for such purposes, Khan emphatically responded, "Absolutely not," signaling his government's firm rejection of any such request.

This declaration was seen as a bold stance in the context of Pakistan's historically complex relationship with the U.S., particularly given Pakistan's past cooperation with the U.S. military during the War on Terror. By rejecting the possibility of allowing U.S. forces to use Pakistani soil for future operations, Khan portrayed himself as a leader  determined to safeguard Pakistan's sovereignty and independence in foreign policy decisions.

Symbol of Sovereignty and Independence

Khan's **"Absolutely Not"** resonated deeply with many Pakistanis who felt that Pakistan had too often been subservient to foreign powers, particularly the U.S. His statement was seen as a rejection of the idea that Pakistan should be used as a tool in foreign conflicts or dictated to by external powers. It became a symbol of his broader push for an independent foreign policy, one that prioritized Pakistan's national interests over those of global superpowers.

Khan had long been critical of Pakistan's involvement in the U.S.-led War on Terror, arguing that it had cost Pakistan immensely in terms of lives, resources, and internal stability. The "Absolutely Not" statement reflected his stance that Pakistan would no longer be drawn into foreign wars or allow its territory to be used for such purposes under his leadership.

Popularization and Political Symbol

The phrase quickly became a rallying cry for Khan's supporters, encapsulating his image as a leader who stood up to foreign pressure. It was widely shared on social media, repeated in political rallies, and used to emphasize Khan's commitment to Pakistan's sovereignty. For many, it represented a turning point in Pakistan's foreign policy — a shift from dependency on the U.S. to a more autonomous, self-reliant approach.

Opposition parties, while critical of Khan on other fronts, found it difficult to challenge the popularity of this phrase, as it struck a chord with nationalist sentiments across the country. The phrase became more than just a refusal to the U.S.; it symbolized a broader assertion of Pakistan's dignity and the desire to chart its own course in international affairs.

6. The Future: A New Political Consciousness

The awakening of public consciousness in Pakistan, driven by Imran Khan's leadership, represents a fundamental shift in the country's political trajectory. Whether Khan returns to power or not, the impact of his movement is likely to be long-lasting. He has galvanized a population that had long been disillusioned with politics and has created a new political consciousness that will continue to shape Pakistan's future.

Khan's legacy will be defined not just by his policies, but by his ability to awaken a sense of self-respect, sovereignty, and justice among the people of Pakistan. His vision of an independent, self-reliant Pakistan has resonated with millions, and even as political dynamics shift, this awakening will remain a powerful force in the nation's collective psyche.

The unprecedented support for Imran Khan—whether seen as a political wave or a broader social movement—marks a turning point in Pakistan's history. It signifies a rejection of the old ways of doing politics and an embrace of a new, more engaged and empowered citizenry. Whether Khan's vision for Pakistan is fully realized or not, the awakening he has sparked will undoubtedly leave a lasting imprint on the country's political landscape.

The Unbroken Spirit of Resistance

Imran Khan, once Pakistan's charismatic prime minister and a symbol of hope for millions, now finds himself in solitary confinement—one of the most isolating and dehumanizing forms of imprisonment. For over a year since May 9, 2023, he has been subjected to confinement, physical and psychological torment, and political persecution by the very forces that once sought to control him. Yet, despite facing immense pressure, relentless attacks, and a variety of fascist tactics aimed at breaking his spirit, Imran Khan has remained steadfast, his resolve unbroken.

The Fall from Power

Imran Khan's journey from the prime minister's office to solitary confinement was swift and brutal. His tenure as Pakistan's leader was marked by promises of reform, anti-corruption efforts, and a vision of a "Naya Pakistan" (New Pakistan), but it also collided headfirst with the entrenched political elite and military establishment that had long dominated the country.

Khan's refusal to toe the line of the traditional power brokers, his criticisms of foreign influence, and his appeal to the masses in his fight for sovereignty, quickly turned him from a political ally to an enemy of the establishment. After a dramatic no-confidence vote in April 2022, Khan was ousted from power in what many have described as a politically motivated coup, orchestrated by corrupt generals, politicians, and foreign powers who saw his nationalist and anti-establishment stance as a threat to their control.

But Khan's removal was just the beginning. What followed was a campaign of harassment, vilification, and imprisonment aimed at silencing him and crushing his growing popularity. Despite the immense pressure, Khan refused to yield to the forces seeking to erase him from the political landscape.

The Fascist Tactics: A Campaign of Suppression

The Pakistan military and political establishment, determined to break Khan's defiance, resorted to a variety of fascist tactics designed not only to eliminate his political influence but also to physically and mentally break him. From the moment of his ousting, the authorities unleashed a wave of repression. Political rallies and public gatherings were banned, media outlets were censored, and Khan's supporters faced intimidation and violence.

One of the most chilling aspects of Khan's imprisonment has been the widespread censorship, particularly his near-total erasure from the public sphere. For months, government authorities imposed strict bans on his image, his name, and even any references to him in the media. Social media accounts supporting him were shut down or monitored, and state-run television channels avoided any coverage of him, turning the airwaves into a one-sided propaganda tool of the establishment.

Despite these oppressive measures, Khan's supporters, many of whom are young and tech-savvy, took to digital platforms with unparalleled fervor. Social media platforms became the last bastion of free speech and dissent, with Khan's loyalists creating viral campaigns and defying the bans on his image. The youth, disillusioned with the political status quo, rallied behind him in massive numbers, refusing to be silenced.

However, the military's power to act without accountability in the country allowed for an escalation of fascist tactics. Khan was arrested multiple times, with his political activity consistently disrupted. The authorities even went so far as to imprison him in solitary confinement—an isolation meant to crush any remaining hope. Solitary confinement is a known form of psychological warfare, meant to break the spirit of the prisoner and make them question their cause. For over a year, Khan has faced this harsh reality, confined to a small, bare cell with little human contact or psychological support.

The Struggle for Survival: Mental and Physical Torture

Imran Khan's time in solitary confinement has not only been a political and legal battle but a brutal test of his mental and physical endurance. The isolation is designed to wear down even the strongest individuals. Deprived of meaningful social contact, access to information, or any form of entertainment, Khan has been left in a stark and oppressive environment. The constant threat of physical harm, intimidation, and political persecution has made his situation even more precarious.

Despite these unimaginable conditions, Khan has remained defiant. His spirit, fortified by years of struggle as a cricket star and political outsider, has proven to be a source of unyielding resistance. Rather than succumbing to the isolation, Khan used his time in confinement to reflect, strengthen his resolve, and continue his fight for the people of Pakistan.

His mental resilience became an inspiration to millions. Inside his cell, Khan refused to be broken. His will to continue the struggle against a corrupt system remained undeterred, and the more the authorities sought to isolate him, the more his message resonated with the masses.

During his confinement, Khan managed to communicate with his supporters through various means, sending out messages of hope and resistance. These messages, often smuggled out through his legal team or via covert channels, served as a rallying cry for his followers. In his absence, the Pakistani people, particularly the youth, organized protests, social media campaigns, and demonstrations. His slogan, "Naya Pakistan," became a symbol of defiance against the corrupt ruling elite and the military-industrial complex that sought to suppress him.

The Growing Pressure: A National Movement

While Khan faced mounting pressure from the military and political elites, the movement he sparked began to grow stronger. His removal from power may have diminished his direct influence, but it gave rise to an unprecedented public uprising. Across Pakistan, his supporters, especially the youth, took to the streets to demand his release and the restoration of democratic principles.

The demand for Khan's freedom became a national cause. Protests erupted in every major city, from Karachi to Lahore to Peshawar. Even in the strongholds of his political rivals, the Pakistan People's Party (PPP) and the Pakistan Muslim League-Nawaz (PML-N), Khan found support. People from all walks of life—workers, students, and intellectuals—came together in solidarity, uniting under a shared belief in justice and fairness.

The military's efforts to break Khan were complicated by the growing public sympathy for him. As the protests intensified, it became increasingly difficult for the establishment to suppress them without risking even more widespread unrest. Pakistan's streets became battlegrounds for a much larger ideological war—one that transcended Khan himself and became a symbol of resistance against the authoritarian forces ruling the country.

The global attention that Imran Khan received during his imprisonment also played a significant role in keeping the pressure on the military and political establishment. International organizations, human rights groups, and foreign governments began to speak out against the undemocratic actions being taken against him. They condemned his arbitrary detention, the suppression of dissent, and the violations of his basic rights, which brought further embarrassment to the Pakistani government and military on the global stage.

The Unbroken Spirit of Imran Khan

Despite everything—the isolation, the constant threats, the media blackout, and the fascist tactics designed to break his resolve—Imran Khan has emerged as a symbol of resistance. Rather than allowing the system to dictate his narrative, Khan has used his time in solitary confinement to forge a stronger bond with his supporters and to continue his fight for the future of Pakistan.

The resilience he has shown during this difficult time is a testament to his indomitable spirit. For those who have stood by him, Khan has become a martyr of sorts, a figure of hope who refuses to be silenced by the machinery of state oppression. The very tactics used to destroy him have only solidified his status as a leader of the people, elevating his stature as a political figure beyond what it ever was when he was in power.

The arrest and continued confinement of Imran Khan might have been intended to extinguish his influence, but it has only fueled his cause. His story has become a rallying cry for those seeking to reclaim Pakistan from corruption, authoritarianism, and foreign control. In the end, the fascist tactics meant to isolate and break him have failed—Khan remains unbroken, a leader still capable of leading the resistance for a new and better Pakistan.

Conclusion: A Movement That Cannot Be Silenced

Imran Khan's time in solitary confinement may have been one of the darkest chapters in his life, but it has also been a testament to his unyielding resolve. The more the military and political establishment sought to break him, the stronger the movement for his freedom became. His spirit, undaunted by the years of oppression, has become the symbol of a nation that refuses to submit to corruption and dictatorship.

Imran Khan's enduring influence and the widespread support for his cause demonstrate that even in the face of state violence and fascist tactics, the will of the people can never be fully extinguished. His struggle is far from over, and as the demand for justice continues to grow, it is clear that his message will live on—unbroken, uncompromised, and ever more powerful in the hearts of those fighting for a better future for Pakistan.

Asim's Assault on Democracy and the Military

The rise of authoritarianism in Pakistan is not a new phenomenon. The nation has witnessed military coups, political repression, and systemic corruption since its inception. However, What began under General Qamar Bajwa and is now unfolding under General Asim Munir may well go down in history as one of the most brazen assaults on democracy in Pakistan, constitutionalism, and even the very institution he is meant to protect—the military. The military, which has long held a dominant influence over the country's political landscape, has now shifted from behind-the-scenes manipulation to outright authoritarian control, threatening the very foundation of democratic governance. Through a calculated mix of constitutional manipulation, coercion, and fear, Asim has set in motion a series of actions that threaten to dismantle the very fabric of Pakistan's democratic system and undermine the credibility of the military itself.

At the core of this unraveling lies the controversial 26th Amendment, a recent constitutional change that seeks to neutralize parliament and strip it of its power, ultimately placing the military in a position of unchallenged supremacy. The amendment, designed to bypass parliamentary authority, centralizes political power in the hands of the military and weakens the judiciary's ability to hold those in power accountable. The consequences of such an amendment would be catastrophic for democratic governance, but the methods employed to push this agenda forward have exposed the fascist tactics of Asim's regime.

Neutralizing Parliament: The 26th Amendment

The 26th Amendment, recently passed under Asim's directive, is the culmination of years of efforts to tighten the military's grip on Pakistan's political system. By limiting the powers of elected representatives and transferring much of their authority to the executive, particularly to military leadership, this amendment aims to transform parliament into a rubber-stamp institution. This move effectively renders elected officials powerless, giving the military unchecked control over critical decisions related to national security, economic policy, and foreign relations.

Under the guise of "national security" and "stability," Asim and his allies have framed the 26th Amendment as a necessary step to protect the country from political chaos. In reality, it is a power grab that sidelines the democratic institutions that were designed to provide checks and balances in the governance of Pakistan.

The Attack on the Judiciary

In parallel with the neutralization of parliament, Asim's regime has also made moves to subdue the judiciary. A special court is being established with the explicit purpose of undermining the independence of judges and controlling the judicial process. This court, staffed by individuals loyal to the regime, is set to handle cases that challenge the military's authority or interfere with its agenda.

The judiciary in Pakistan, while historically flawed, has played a pivotal role in holding power to account. Under Asim's regime, judges who have dared to oppose the military or question the legality of the amendment have been threatened, harassed, and in some cases, removed from their positions. The goal is clear: to create a judiciary that is entirely subservient to the military, where the rule of law is replaced by the rule of fear.

Tactics of Terror: Abduction, Torture, and Bribery

The passage of the 26th Amendment has not been without significant resistance. Members of parliament who have opposed the amendment, along with those within the judiciary who have spoken out, have faced a chilling campaign of coercion. In a grim reminder of the worst days of authoritarianism, family members of dissenting politicians have been abducted, tortured, and held hostage as a means of silencing opposition. These tactics are not only a direct violation of human rights but also a reflection of the desperation of Asim's regime to quash any resistance to their agenda.

In addition to these violent measures, the regime has resorted to bribery and corruption on a massive scale. Parliamentarians have been offered exorbitant sums of money to switch their votes in favor of the amendment, while others have been threatened with fabricated legal cases, imprisonment, and worse if they fail to comply. The use of financial incentives, combined with the ever-present threat of violence, has created an atmosphere of terror within the corridors of power.

Those who dare to defy the regime face not only political ruin but personal destruction. Some parliamentarians have gone into hiding, while others have capitulated under the immense pressure. What was once a diverse and active legislature is now being hollowed out by a regime determined to enforce its will through intimidation.

By weakening the role of elected representatives and the judiciary, the amendment threatens to reduce Pakistan's democratic experiment to a mere facade. **The public, particularly the younger generation, is increasingly disillusioned with a system that appears to prioritize the interests of a few powerful elites over the welfare of the people.** This political siege, orchestrated through the amendment, has further deepened the divide between the state and its citizens, eroding trust in democratic governance.

A Betrayal of the Military and the Nation

What makes Asim's actions even more egregious is his **betrayal of the very institution he was meant to serve: the military.** The Pakistan Army has long been a symbol of national pride and security, but under Asim's leadership, it has been transformed into a tool of political oppression. By engaging in power plays and eroding the military's once-esteemed reputation, Asim is actively working against the interests of Pakistan's military, country, and its people.

In pursuing his authoritarian agenda, Asim has dragged the military into the political mud, exposing it to criticism and mistrust from both the public and international observers. His actions have damaged the image of the armed forces, reducing them from defenders of the nation to enforcers of a corrupt and self-serving regime. **The very institution that once stood as a guardian of Pakistan's sovereignty is now seen as a force of** repression, used to suppress democratic freedoms and silence opposition.

Serving Foreign Masters

Adding another layer to the treachery, **Asim's agenda appears to serve not just his personal ambitions but also the interests of foreign powers.** Rather than protecting Pakistan's sovereignty and prioritizing the needs of its people, he has aligned himself with external actors who seek to influence Pakistan's internal affairs for their own strategic goals. The manipulation of Pakistan's democratic institutions, the weakening of its economy, and the erosion of its military's credibility all serve to destabilize the country, leaving it vulnerable to foreign influence.

Asim's regime, in exchange for political and financial support, seems more than willing to compromise Pakistan's independence. This betrayal of national interests in favor of appeasing foreign masters has sparked outrage among Pakistan's patriots, many of whom see Asim's actions as a grave threat to the country's future. Instead of defending Pakistan from external threats, Asim's policies are actively weakening the nation and exposing it to exploitation by foreign powers.

A Nation Held Hostage

For ordinary Pakistanis, the effects of Asim's fascist tactics are deeply felt. The suppression of political dissent, combined with the crackdown on the media and the erosion of civil liberties, has plunged the country into a state of fear. Journalists are imprisoned for reporting the truth, activists are detained without due process, and peaceful protests are met with brutal force. The once-vibrant civil society in Pakistan is being systematically dismantled, leaving citizens with little recourse to challenge the abuses of power.

Furthermore, the regime's heavy-handed tactics have stifled economic growth, alienated international allies, and exacerbated social divisions. As the military continues to consolidate its power, Pakistan finds itself increasingly isolated on the world stage. Countries that once supported Pakistan's democratic development now look on with concern as the nation slides deeper into authoritarianism.

The Legacy of a Dictator

History is replete with the names of dictators who, through their ruthless pursuit of power, left indelible marks of cruelty and oppression. General Asim's name is poised to join this infamous list. By employing fascist tactics to dismantle Pakistan's democratic institutions and erode the reputation of the military, he is positioning himself not only as a strongman but as a dictator whose reign will be remembered for its brutality and betrayal.

As General Asim's authoritarianism continues to deepen, the military's reputation has suffered irreparable damage. No longer seen as the protector of the state, it is now viewed as an instrument of oppression, working against the interests of the nation while serving foreign masters. This internal assault has created a dangerous fracture within the institution, with some members quietly questioning the legitimacy of their leadership's actions.

The legacy of Asim's rule will be one of division and destruction, where the voice of the people was silenced in the name of security, and where the promise of democracy was sacrificed for the preservation of military dominance. His actions are not just an affront to Pakistan's constitution but a betrayal of the very principles on which the nation was founded.

The Road Ahead

As General Asim's authoritarianism continues to deepen, the military's reputation has suffered irreparable damage. No longer seen as the protector of the state, it is now viewed as an instrument of oppression, working against the interests of the nation while serving foreign masters. This internal assault has created a dangerous fracture within the institution, with some members quietly questioning the legitimacy of their leadership's actions.

In the long run, Asim's assault on democracy may prove to be a turning point in Pakistan's history. Whether it leads to the complete militarization of the state or sparks a resistance movement that reignites the democratic spirit of the nation, the implications will shape Pakistan's political landscape for generations to come.

For now, Asim Munir's regime stands as a dark chapter in Pakistan's journey, one that will be remembered for its ruthlessness, its betrayal of democratic principles, and its reckless disregard for the people it was meant to serve.

The road ahead is uncertain, but one thing is clear: Asim's legacy will be written in the annals of history, not as a leader who protected Pakistan, but as a cruel dictator who brought the nation to the brink of ruin and tarnished the military's standing in the process.

Asim Munir at a crossroads with Imran Khan

Asim Munir's tenure has been marked by an escalating personal grudge, antagonism, and hostility towards Imran Khan, which many believe has transcended professional boundaries and is now impacting Pakistan's political landscape and sovereignty. This deep-seated animosity appears to stem from past conflicts, as Khan's government removed Munir from his post as ISI chief in 2019, creating a personal rift that has since grown into open rivalry. Munir's actions, viewed by some as politically motivated, have contributed to a heightened military involvement in civilian affairs, undermining the democratic process and weakening the independence of institutions. His efforts to marginalize Khan, whether through legal battles or attempts to discredit him politically, are seen as fueling instability within the country. Critics argue that such actions are detrimental to Pakistan's sovereignty, as they divert focus from critical national issues, disrupt democratic governance, and weaken public trust in both the military and civilian leadership. Alarmingly, Munir's actions seem to be aiding the enemies of Pakistan by creating internal division and chaos. Some even suggest that he is "dancing to their tunes," as his focus on settling personal scores with Khan distracts from Pakistan's real challenges, making the country more vulnerable to external threats. This internal power struggle risks destabilizing the nation's political fabric, with broader consequences for Pakistan's future security and sovereignty.

The relationship between General Asim Munir and Imran Khan has placed both individuals at a significant crossroads in Pakistan's political and military landscape. Their paths have been intricately intertwined as the former head of Pakistan's intelligence services and the current Chief of Army Staff (COAS), Munir, grapples with a political crisis where Imran Khan stands as the central figure of opposition. Here are the key dynamics at play between the two leaders:

1. Military-Political Tensions:

Asim Munir, as the COAS, inherits a military institution that has historically played a dominant role in Pakistan's politics. Since assuming his role, Munir faces immense pressure to stabilize the country's political landscape, where the military is both a major player and an arbiter in national affairs. His predecessor's influence, coupled with the military's past involvement in backing political figures, including Imran Khan's rise to power in 2018, puts Munir in a difficult position.

Imran Khan, ousted from office in 2022, has made a powerful political comeback, largely based on his critique of military interference in politics. His ouster, widely seen as orchestrated by political opponents with alleged military backing, has left him in direct confrontation with the establishment. His ongoing popularity, despite facing legal challenges and incarceration, continues to make him a major political force, complicating the military's efforts to manage the country's political trajectory.

2. The May 9th Drama:

One of the most pivotal and controversial moments in the standoff between Asim Munir and Imran Khan occurred on May 9, 2023, following Khan's arrest. The aftermath of that day is widely seen as a defining moment in Pakistan's recent political history, and for many, it was a turning point that deepened the confrontation between the military and the PTI. However, there are widespread suspicions that the violence on May 9th may have been an insider job orchestrated by Pakistan's intelligence agencies, designed to frame Imran Khan and his party to justify a broader crackdown on PTI.

For General Asim Munir, the events of May 9th presented both an opportunity and a dilemma. On one hand, it allowed the military to take a firmer stance against the PTI, reinforcing its authority and taking action against what it presented as an unruly political force. On the other hand, the widespread public skepticism about the true nature of the events has placed Munir and the military leadership in a difficult position.

The intelligence agencies' role in the crackdown, and the rapid framing of Imran Khan, raised suspicions that Munir was complicit in orchestrating the narrative against the PTI. The military's swift response, which included not only mass arrests but also the detention of key PTI leaders and censorship of Khan's name and image, made it clear that the establishment was fully prepared to use the May 9th violence as a justification for a broader offensive against Khan's movement.

However, this approach has also backfired in several ways. The harsh crackdown, coupled with the allegations of an insider job, has led to a significant erosion of public trust in the military.

Even as the intelligence agencies tried to control the narrative, social media became a battleground where PTI supporters quickly debunked official stories, further complicating the military's efforts to shape public perception.

3. Public Skepticism and the Military's Dilemma

Despite the military's efforts to present May 9th as a spontaneous outbreak of PTI-led violence, public skepticism remains high. Many believe that the intelligence agencies and sections of the military orchestrated the violence to frame Imran Khan and dismantle his political movement. This narrative has gained traction on social media, where the PTI's "social media tigers" continue to counter the military's version of events with alternative explanations and evidence.

For Asim Munir, the events of May 9th have placed him at a crossroads. While the military has long been seen as the ultimate power broker in Pakistan, its credibility is now under threat. By relying on heavy-handed tactics, including the repression of PTI and the muzzling of dissent, the military risks alienating the public further and deepening the political crisis.

4. The Imran Khan Factor:

Imran Khan represents a unique challenge for Munir because of his unparalleled popularity and ability to mobilize the masses, despite being jailed and isolated. The military's traditional strategy of sidelining political figures through arrests or coercion has not worked effectively in Khan's case. His celebrity status, coupled with his narrative of resistance against foreign interference and military overreach, has only strengthened his political capital.

Khan's continued ability to command loyalty from his supporters, even from prison, leaves Munir with limited options. The military's usual strategies of silencing dissent and controlling opposition leaders are proving ineffective. Even within the ranks of the establishment, there are reported fractures, with some factions possibly sympathetic to Khan's populist message.

5. The Crossroads: Course Correction or Continued Confrontation?

General Asim Munir faces a critical decision. Continuing with repressive tactics, possibly underpinned by the intelligence agencies' actions on May 9th, may provide short-term control but will likely fuel long-term unrest. The public's distrust of the military has reached new heights, and Imran Khan's popularity, even in the face of arrests and media bans, remains undiminished. This leaves the military with few options other than further repression, which risks plunging the country into greater instability.

The military under Munir has the opportunity to recalibrate its relationship with Pakistan's civilian leadership. A course correction—which might involve a return to a more neutral role, allowing civilian politics to function independently—could stabilize the situation and possibly restore some public faith in the military. However, this would require Munir and the military leadership to step back from decades of political interference.

On the other hand, if Munir chooses continued confrontation, it could lead to a protracted period of unrest, further polarizing the country and eroding the military's standing as a respected institution. With Khan's political resilience and the inability of the state to control his narrative, this route is fraught with risks.

6. Impact on Pakistan's Stability:

Pakistan's political stability is closely tied to how this standoff between Munir and Khan unfolds. The military, having traditionally maintained its dominance, finds itself at risk of losing influence if it cannot manage the Imran Khan phenomenon. Any misstep—such as an escalation of repression or, as some fear, an assassination attempt on Khan—could plunge Pakistan into chaos, further destabilizing the country both politically and economically.

Asim Munir must also consider international pressure. Pakistan's global allies are closely watching how the military handles the political crisis, particularly with concerns about democracy, human rights, and regional stability. Any harsh measures that are perceived as undermining democratic norms could lead to diplomatic and economic consequences, especially in relations with Western nations.

Conclusion:

Asim Munir stands at a defining moment in Pakistan's political history, where his actions could determine not only the future of Imran Khan's political career but also the long-term role of the military in governance. The decisions made in the coming months could either further entrench the military's involvement in politics or lead to a rebalancing of civil-military relations. For now, Imran Khan remains the pivotal figure in this equation, and how Munir navigates this crossroads will have profound implications for Pakistan's stability and democratic future.

The Fight for Democracy–The Fight for Pakistan

As Pakistan drifts further into authoritarianism under General Asim's regime, the fight for democracy has become a critical struggle for the nation's future. The battle is no longer between political ideologies but between the forces of oppression and those who stand for justice and freedom. In this increasingly polarized environment, Imran Khan's Pakistan Tehreek-e-Insaf (PTI) stands as the only opposition to the current regime, as all other major political parties have aligned themselves with the military in exchange for power. The struggle for Pakistan's democratic future now rests on the shoulders of a determined few—chief among them the nation's youth.

PTI: The Only Opposition Standing

In the political vacuum created by General Asim's tightening grip on power, Imran Khan and PTI have emerged as the last line of defense for democracy in Pakistan. Other political entities, once vocal in their criticisms of military interference, have now chosen to sit comfortably in the military's lap, trading democratic principles for political survival. In stark contrast, PTI has refused to bow to the pressure, positioning itself as the sole opposition to the current regime.

Khan's ousting from power in 2022, which his supporters call a product of international conspiracies and domestic manipulation, marked the beginning of a new phase in his political journey. His message of justice, accountability, and reform resonates more strongly than ever with a disillusioned populace, and his survival of multiple assassination attempts has only elevated his status as a symbol of resistance. Despite intense repression, PTI continues to organize protests, mobilize supporters, and challenge the regime through legal avenues, standing firm in the face of an increasingly hostile state.

Civil Society: A Silence That Speaks Volumes

While civil society has traditionally played a crucial role in defending democracy, its response to the current wave of repression has been muted. Human rights organizations, legal bodies, and activists have largely retreated, perhaps cowed by the regime's brutal tactics, including abductions, torture, and extrajudicial detentions. The relative silence of civil society is one of the most tragic aspects of the current struggle. Those who remain vocal face swift retribution from a regime that will not tolerate dissent.

A hallmark of this repression has been the abduction and torture of journalists, PTI workers, and ordinary citizens by intelligence personnel in vehicles infamously known as **Vigo dala**. With covered faces, these operatives abduct individuals without presenting any legal warrants or justifications. Many of the abducted individuals are subjected to torture and inhumane treatment, leaving deep psychological and physical scars. The sheer impunity with which these operations are conducted has instilled a climate of fear and intimidation, silencing dissent through terror.

Despite this, some courageous individuals within civil society continue to fight. Lawyers, once pivotal in restoring Pakistan's judiciary, are again rising to challenge special courts that seek to undermine judicial independence. They are at the forefront of legal battles to defend Pakistan's democratic values, yet their voices are often drowned out by the overwhelming silence.

The Youth: The Beating Heart of the Resistance

In the vacuum left by a largely silent civil society, it is the youth of Pakistan, who represent over 60 percent of the population, that have become the symbol of resistance. This young, energetic demographic, which had once hoped for a future built on democratic principles, now finds itself standing against a system determined to crush their dreams. Disillusioned by years of corruption, military overreach, and economic stagnation, the youth see in Imran Khan not just a political leader, but a symbol of their own fight for a better Pakistan.

Students, activists, and young professionals have taken to the streets, organized on social media, and formed networks of resistance. Despite the regime's efforts to silence them—through censorship, arrests, abductions, and violence—their spirit remains unbroken. For many of them, the fight for democracy is personal: it is a fight for the future they wish to inherit. PTI's youth-led movements have managed to keep the hope for a democratic Pakistan alive, even as General Asim's regime tightens its grip on the nation.

Media: Truth in the Crosshairs

The media, long seen as a guardian of truth and a check on power, is now under siege. Independent journalists face harassment, imprisonment, or worse, as the regime cracks down on any form of dissent. Major news outlets, once free to report on corruption and human rights abuses, have been muzzled or brought under state control. Those who dare to speak out face dire consequences, and many have been forced into silence or exile.

Journalists, too, have been among the **victims of the infamous Vigo dala abductions**, snatched from their homes or workplaces in the dead of night. Many have been held without charges, their families left in the dark about their whereabouts. The message is clear: challenge the regime, and you will be silenced. Yet, despite the fear, many independent journalists continue to operate in the shadows, risking their lives to expose the truth.

Diaspora and International Advocacy

The Pakistani diaspora has also become a crucial force in the fight for democracy. From London to New York, to the Gulf states, expatriate Pakistanis are organizing protests, lobbying governments, and raising awareness about the human rights violations taking place in their homeland. Their efforts have put international pressure on the regime and drawn the attention of global human rights organizations.

Amnesty International, Human Rights Watch, and other organizations have been vocal in their condemnation of the crackdown on free speech, political persecution, and the military's role in propping up Asim's authoritarian rule. While geopolitical realities complicate foreign governments' responses, especially given Pakistan's strategic importance, international scrutiny has nonetheless forced the regime to face growing global criticism.

The Erosion of the Military's Reputation

What is particularly destructive about General Asim's rule is how it has damaged the reputation of Pakistan's military—an institution long regarded as the nation's defender. Under Asim's leadership, the military has become embroiled in political machinations, resulting in a loss of credibility both within Pakistan and abroad. Once a symbol of national pride and protection, the military is now seen by many as a tool of oppression, serving foreign interests rather than protecting the sovereignty of the country.

Asim's actions have not only harmed the military's standing but have also divided its ranks, with growing discontent among mid-level officers and soldiers who question the role they are being asked to play in repressing their fellow citizens. By using the military to maintain his grip on power, Asim is working against the military's true mission: to serve and protect the nation. Instead, he is subverting its purpose, damaging its honor, and driving it to work against the very people it was sworn to defend.

Conclusion: A Nation at the Crossroads

Pakistan today stands at a crossroads. The fight for democracy is no longer just about politics; it is about the survival of the nation itself. PTI remains the only political force resisting the regime, and it is the youth of Pakistan who have emerged as the vanguard of this struggle. Their fight is not just for a return to democratic norms but for a future that promises justice, accountability, and opportunity for all.

General Asim's regime, through its tactics of oppression, censorship, and brutality, may appear unbreakable. But history has shown that the will of the people, when united, can overcome even the most entrenched systems of authoritarianism. As Pakistanis continue their struggle, both at home and abroad, the hope for a democratic and just Pakistan remains alive. The fight for democracy is not just a political battle—it is the fight for Pakistan itself.

If Military Dare to Assassinate Khan - Directly or Indirectly?

In the tumultuous political landscape of Pakistan, one name stands as a beacon of defiance against the corrupt establishment: Imran Khan. His unwavering commitment to his vision, his indomitable spirit, and his relentless pursuit of justice have made him not just a politician, but a symbol of hope for millions. However, as Khan continues to challenge the entrenched powers of the military and political elites, the question arises: what if the military dares to assassinate him?

This chapter explores the profound consequences such an act would have on Pakistan—socially, politically, and economically—and why, in many ways, Imran Khan has already won, regardless of the outcome. His life or death, while critical to Pakistan's future, represents more than just a single man's struggle; it signifies a pivotal moment for the country's destiny.

Imran Khan: The Symbol of Hope

Imran Khan is not just the leader of Pakistan Tehreek-e-Insaf (PTI) but the embodiment of a broader movement for justice, accountability, and self-reliance. His life has become synonymous with the fight for a better Pakistan—one that is free from the clutches of corruption, military interference, and the political dynasties that have long held the country hostage. Khan's message of hope, progress, and honesty has resonated deeply with millions of Pakistanis who have grown weary of the status quo.

Khan's unprecedented popularity spans across different demographics, from urban youth to the rural poor, who see in him a savior capable of breaking the chains that have bound Pakistan's progress for decades. His struggles, both personal and political, have made him an icon, and his arrest in May 2023 only solidified his status as the people's champion.

His fight against the military's involvement in politics, against the corrupt political system, and against foreign manipulation of Pakistan's resources has made him a polarizing figure. But no matter the level of controversy or the degree of personal attacks, Khan's ability to inspire and mobilize millions is undeniable. His position as a political outsider, untainted by the system that has led Pakistan to ruin, makes him the last hope for those seeking change.

The Unthinkable: The Assassination of Imran Khan

The prospect of the military targeting Imran Khan for assassination is one that sends tremors through the nation. Pakistan's history is riddled with military-led coups, political assassinations, and covert operations aimed at silencing dissent. In recent years, as Imran Khan's political movement gained momentum, the military's efforts to maintain control over Pakistan's governance became more overt and ruthless.

If the unthinkable were to occur—if Khan were to be assassinated by the very forces that seek to suppress him—the shockwaves would be felt across Pakistan and beyond. While such an act may momentarily silence Khan and his supporters, the repercussions would be far-reaching and irreversible. The question is no longer just about Imran Khan's life or death—it is about the future of the entire nation.

The Nation's Reaction: Unprecedented Unrest

Imran Khan's death at the hands of the military would unleash a level of public outcry and civil unrest that Pakistan has never seen. Khan has garnered unprecedented support from all corners of society, and his martyrdom would transform him from a political leader into a national icon. The millions of Pakistanis who have supported his cause would see his death as the ultimate betrayal by the military establishment—an act that confirms the very corruption and authoritarianism he spent his life fighting against.

The streets of Pakistan would likely explode with protests, as people from all walks of life pour into the streets to mourn their leader and demand justice. The military, which already faces significant internal and external pressure due to its role in

Pakistan's political and economic crisis, would find itself grappling with a nationwide uprising that could destabilize the entire country.

Civil disobedience, strikes, and violent protests would likely erupt, plunging Pakistan into a state of anarchy. The military, which has relied on authoritarian control for decades, would find itself facing a population that is no longer willing to be controlled by force or fear. The assassination of Khan would not only ignite a popular revolt but could also spark a series of political shifts that could irreparably fracture Pakistan's power structure.

A Nation on the Brink: Destabilization and Collapse

The repercussions of Khan's assassination would go beyond mere political instability. Pakistan is already on the brink of an economic collapse, and the loss of its most charismatic and popular leader could push the country over the edge. With the public losing faith in both the military and the government, investor confidence would evaporate, exacerbating the country's economic crisis. The nation's already dire financial situation would deteriorate further, with international organizations, foreign investors, and global powers becoming even more wary of engaging with Pakistan.

The military, which already struggles with its credibility, would be seen as the ultimate oppressor in Pakistan's history. In the eyes of millions, the military would no longer be the institution that protects the nation but the force that destroys it. Pakistan's relationship with its citizens would become irrevocably fractured, and the country's future as a unified nation would be in jeopardy.

Moreover, the assassination of Khan would significantly impact Pakistan's foreign relations. The international community would condemn the military's actions, and Pakistan would find itself further isolated on the world stage. Foreign governments, businesses, and organizations would likely distance themselves from a country seen as politically unstable and unable to provide basic governance or security. Pakistan's global standing would plummet, leaving the country in an even more precarious situation.

Imran Khan: Alive or Dead, He Is The Winner

While the consequences of Khan's assassination would be catastrophic for Pakistan, there is a profound truth that the military and other powers seeking to suppress him must recognize: Imran Khan is already a winner, regardless of whether he survives his time in jail or is martyred. The forces that have sought to silence him are fighting a losing battle. Khan's legacy is already cemented in the hearts of millions who see him as a symbol of hope, integrity, and justice. His vision for a just and self-reliant Pakistan has inspired countless individuals to stand against corruption and foreign influence, and his martyrdom would only elevate his status, making him a hero for generations to come. His message has struck a chord with Pakistan's youth, who see in him a path forward, away from the cycle of political dynasties and military dominance. Imran Khan has ignited a fire that cannot be extinguished. His martyrdom would only fuel the flames of revolution, ensuring that his movement continues to grow, regardless of his physical absence.

However, the loss to the country would be immeasurable. The killing of Imran Khan would plunge Pakistan into further instability, deepening political and social divides. His absence would leave a leadership vacuum, and the dreams of a "Naya Pakistan"—one free from corruption and exploitation—could be shattered. The nation, already grappling with economic turmoil and internal strife, would suffer irreparably as trust in democratic processes and justice would further erode.

Imran Khan's vision transcends politics; it's about restoring national dignity, sovereignty, and self-confidence. His assassination would not only rob Pakistan of its last hope for transformative change but also threaten the unity and future of the nation. While Khan's spirit and legacy would endure, the country and its people would pay a heavy price.

If Imran Khan survives the prison sentence and emerges from this trial alive, he will be more powerful than ever. His imprisonment, rather than weakening him, has served to further solidify his status as a symbol of resistance. The public's demand for his release would grow louder, and with it, the resolve to bring about the systemic changes Pakistan so desperately needs. Khan's message would resonate even more strongly, as the masses rally behind him, demanding an end to the military's control over civilian affairs and a restoration of democracy.

Conclusion: The Future of Pakistan Lies with Imran Khan

Imran Khan is not just a leader; he is the embodiment of Pakistan's desire for change, for a future free of corruption and military dictatorship. Whether alive or dead, his influence will continue to shape the destiny of Pakistan. His death could trigger a wave of protests and civil unrest that could destabilize the country, but it would also serve to further his cause.

For the military, the decision to target Imran Khan is a dangerous gamble, one that risks not only his life but the very future of Pakistan. As long as Khan's message resonates with the people, as long as his call for justice echoes in the hearts of millions, Pakistan's future remains tied to him. His movement will not die with him; it will grow, even in his absence.

Pakistan's future is uncertain, but one thing is clear: Imran Khan, whether alive or dead, is the symbol of the change that Pakistan needs. The forces that seek to suppress him cannot stop the tide of history.

Course Correction: The Only Option for the Military

As Pakistan teeters on the edge of political and social instability, the military, which has traditionally held significant sway over the country's governance, faces an undeniable crossroads. The path it chooses in the coming months and years will define not only the future of Pakistan but also the military's place in the nation's history. The need for a course correction has never been more pressing, yet the entrenched mindset of the military leadership—rooted in a sense of infallibility and authoritarian control—presents a significant barrier to change.

The Military's Historical Role in Politics

For decades, Pakistan's military has been the de facto power behind the scenes, controlling not only the defense but also the political and economic levers of the country. With a history of coups, martial law, and military-backed regimes, the army has shaped the country's governance model, often at the expense of civilian institutions and democracy. The military's dominance has perpetuated a cycle of political instability, with frequent interventions in civilian governance, leading to the rise and fall of various governments.

While the military has often justified its interventions as necessary for national security and the stability of the state, this mindset has increasingly led to the erosion of democratic processes. The result has been a weakening of Pakistan's political institutions, chronic economic instability, and the growth of a powerful military-industrial complex that has worked to preserve its own interests rather than the interests of the nation.

The rise of political figures like Imran Khan, who stand firmly against the military's overreach into politics, represents a threat to this entrenched system. Khan's call for a democratic Pakistan, free from military interference, resonates with millions of Pakistanis who are frustrated with decades of mismanagement and authoritarianism. However, the military's resistance to this change is not only damaging to Pakistan's democratic fabric but is also contributing to its overall decline.

The Military's Rigid Mindset: "Might is Right" and "More Loyal Than the Queen"

The military's refusal to adapt to the changing political realities is deeply rooted in its rigid mindset. The belief in "Might is Right"—the idea that the military's power should dictate national decisions—has historically been used to justify authoritarian actions. The military's philosophy of governance has long been built on the idea that it is the ultimate protector of the state, even if that protection comes at the cost of democracy and human rights.

Coupled with this is the "More Loyal Than the Queen" mentality, where military leaders, often seeing themselves as defenders of national interests, go to extreme lengths to ensure the survival of the status quo. This approach involves aligning with powerful external forces, sometimes to the detriment of Pakistan's sovereignty and self-determination. The military has often been willing to subvert national interests to maintain its grip on power or curry favor with foreign powers, particularly when it involves securing military aid or maintaining strategic alliances.

This rigid, authoritarian mindset has alienated the very people the military is meant to serve. As Pakistan's economic and political crises deepen, the military's refusal to embrace change only exacerbates the country's challenges. The increasing alienation of Pakistan's population, particularly the youth, from the military's leadership is creating an environment ripe for unrest and social instability.

The Growing Call for Reform

Imran Khan's rise to power, and his subsequent stance against the military's interference in politics, has highlighted the growing frustration with the military's dominance. His campaign for "Naya Pakistan"—a new Pakistan free from corruption, military interference, and dynastic politics—has resonated with millions, especially the youth, who are disillusioned with the status quo.

The PTI (Pakistan Tehreek-e-Insaf) party under Khan's leadership has become the political force most vocal about the need for a systemic overhaul, including a reduction in military influence in civilian matters. Khan's insistence on democratic accountability and institutional reform, coupled with his calls for an end to political patronage and military domination, has made him the most significant political figure to challenge the military's grip in recent history.

The growing support for Khan's ideas—spanning across different segments of Pakistani society—reflects a deep-seated desire for change. People want a government that is accountable to them, not one that is beholden to military interests. They seek institutions that function independently, where civilian leadership holds the reins of power, and where the military's role is strictly confined to national defense.

The Consequences of Ignoring the Call for Change

If the military continues to resist the call for change and refuses to embrace course correction, the consequences for Pakistan could be dire. The country is already facing an economic crisis, compounded by political instability, social unrest, and a lack of investor confidence. The military's continued dominance in the political sphere has only exacerbated these issues, creating a cycle of corruption, inefficiency, and stagnation.

In this scenario, the military will increasingly find itself at odds with a growing section of the population. The longer it resists reform, the greater the potential for widespread disillusionment and unrest. Public anger, if left unchecked, could boil over into full-scale civil disobedience or protests, destabilizing the nation even further.

Furthermore, the military's refusal to allow a peaceful political transition could leave the country vulnerable to internal conflict or even fragmentation. The increased repression of political opponents, the targeting of journalists, and the stifling of dissent will only foster greater resentment, ultimately undermining the military's authority. As the military faces mounting internal and external pressures, its credibility will continue to erode.

The Need for a Course Correction

For the military leadership, course correction is not just an option; it is an imperative if Pakistan is to have any hope of avoiding total collapse. The military must recognize that its historical dominance in the political sphere has only contributed to the country's deep-rooted issues. The time has come for the military to relinquish its role as the political arbiter and to allow democratic processes to take center stage.

Course correction does not mean abandoning Pakistan's security needs. It means that the military should focus on its core function: defending the nation, while allowing civilian institutions to flourish and take charge of governance. The military must respect the sovereignty of elected governments, ensuring that Pakistan's political system functions without interference.

A real course correction involves embracing democracy, respecting the rule of law, and supporting the growth of democratic institutions. It means recognizing that the power to govern should lie in the hands of the people, through their freely elected representatives, and not in the hands of a military establishment that operates beyond the reach of accountability.

The Path to Reform: Rebuilding Trust and Stability

To begin the process of course correction, the military leadership must first acknowledge the legitimacy of popular demands for reform. This includes ensuring free and fair elections, ending political manipulation, and restoring the independence of Pakistan's judiciary and media. It also means addressing the military's internal corruption, its influence over key industries, and its unchecked control over vast segments of the economy.

For Pakistan to move forward, the military must work with political leaders, civil society, and the people to create an environment where democratic processes are respected, and where the rule of law is upheld. It requires the military to be more transparent in its actions, accountable for its role in governance, and committed to upholding human rights.

By embracing this course correction, the military can help create a stable, democratic Pakistan—a nation where governance is based on accountability, transparency, and the collective will of the people. In turn, this will lead to economic stability, greater international respect, and a future that is brighter for all Pakistanis.

Conclusion: The Military's Last Chance

The military's rigid mindset may have served it in the past, but it is now a liability that threatens to destroy the very fabric of Pakistan. Course correction is not just the only option—it is the last chance for the military to restore its credibility and secure Pakistan's future.

The military must choose to adapt or face the inevitable consequences of its resistance to change. The longer it resists the inevitable, the greater the risk that Pakistan will slip into a state of permanent instability, from which recovery may be impossible. The path to redemption for the military is clear: embrace democratic governance, respect the rule of law, and ensure that Pakistan's future is led by its people, not by the power of the military. The choice is theirs, but the stakes are too high for further delay.

How Global Powers Stand to Gain from Imran Khan's Return

Imran Khan's return to power holds profound significance not just for Pakistan, but for global powers with vested interests in South Asia. In a world where geopolitical stability is increasingly interconnected, a stable, prosperous Pakistan under Imran Khan's leadership would yield benefits that extend far beyond the nation's borders. His track record of advocating for justice, anti-corruption, and regional stability positions him as a leader capable of reshaping Pakistan in a way that aligns with the strategic, economic, and security interests of both regional and global powers.

A stable Pakistan, underpinned by Khan's vision of a transparent, accountable government, will help address longstanding issues of terrorism, economic instability, and corruption—creating a more favorable environment for international collaboration, trade, and security. For global powers, including the U.S., China, Russia, Gulf States, and the European Union, Khan's leadership offers an opportunity to solidify Pakistan's role as a reliable partner in the region.

1. Regional Stability: Securing South Asia for Global Peace

Imran Khan's approach to governance, focusing on security and internal stability, would directly benefit global powers by helping to stabilize South Asia, a region often marked by volatility. Khan's return would likely enhance border security, especially with Afghanistan, where the West, China, and Russia have long-term interests in maintaining peace following years of conflict. By curbing terrorism and extremist movements within Pakistan, Khan can contribute to a more secure regional environment, which in turn reduces the threat of terrorism reaching other nations.

His peace-building initiatives, including past efforts to engage in dialogue with neighboring countries like India, also suggest that Khan could help de-escalate tensions in one of the world's most volatile regions. For global powers with economic and security stakes in South Asia, a more peaceful Pakistan ensures that the region doesn't become a breeding ground for terrorism or international conflict.

2. Economic Growth: A Gateway to Global Markets

A Pakistan under Khan's leadership offers significant economic opportunities for global players. Khan has been a strong advocate for economic reform, focusing on transparency, reducing corruption, and creating a business-friendly environment. Global powers, particularly those with strong commercial interests like China, the U.S., and the Gulf countries, stand to benefit from a stable and prosperous Pakistan that serves as a gateway to South Asian and Central Asian markets.

Khan's commitment to infrastructure development, enhancing exports, and fostering foreign direct investment will attract businesses from across the world. The China-Pakistan Economic Corridor (CPEC) will remain a cornerstone of Pakistan's economic landscape, providing China with a crucial trade route and access to the Arabian Sea. However, Khan's return could also balance Pakistan's relations with the West, making room for other powers to engage in trade and investment in a more transparent and stable economy.

Global corporations could find a burgeoning market in Pakistan's growing middle class, while new reforms could open doors for investments in technology, energy, and other sectors vital to the global economy. Khan's efforts to revive Pakistan's economy would bring long-term benefits to the international community, creating a mutually beneficial landscape for trade and development.

3. Climate Action and Sustainability: A Global Priority

Imran Khan's environmental initiatives, including the "Billion Tree Tsunami" and his focus on sustainable development, align with global concerns about climate change. Pakistan, as one of the countries most vulnerable to climate-related disasters, has a critical role to play in international efforts to combat global warming. Under Khan's leadership, the country could become a key partner for global powers in environmental conservation and renewable energy projects.

By fostering international cooperation on climate initiatives, Pakistan could attract green investments and support from Western nations and global financial institutions. This would not only enhance Pakistan's capacity to deal with climate-related issues but also position it as a leader in South Asia's environmental movement. A stable Pakistan under Khan could help accelerate global progress on climate change, providing a model for sustainable development in the region.

4. Geopolitical Leverage: A Key Player in Global Power Dynamics

Imran Khan's return to power could reshape Pakistan's geopolitical role, benefiting multiple global powers who seek influence in South Asia. Khan has always pursued an independent foreign policy, balancing relations between China, the West, and the Middle East. His ability to navigate complex international relationships would allow global powers to engage with Pakistan more effectively, securing their strategic interests without being overly reliant on one-sided allegiances.

For Western powers, Khan's leadership would provide a critical ally in counterbalancing China's growing influence in the region. Simultaneously, Khan's pragmatic approach to China's Belt and Road Initiative, particularly CPEC, could ensure that Pakistan continues to benefit from Chinese investments while maintaining strategic autonomy. Global powers like Russia and the Gulf nations could also find opportunities to strengthen their ties with Pakistan, fostering greater cooperation on energy, defense, and technology.

5. Restoring Democratic Values and Rule of Law

Global powers that prioritize democratic governance and human rights would find a natural ally in Imran Khan. His fight against entrenched corruption and his efforts to strengthen Pakistan's democratic institutions would provide a counterbalance to authoritarianism and military dominance. For countries that value democratic principles, Khan's return represents an opportunity to support a government committed to transparency, justice, and accountability.

This alignment with global democratic values would encourage international investments, partnerships, and cooperation in various sectors. Khan's leadership would also ensure that Pakistan remains an important player in the global discourse on human rights, peace-building, and good governance, benefiting global powers interested in promoting democratic stability across the world.

6. Counterterrorism and Extremism: A Partner for Global Security

Imran Khan's moderate Islamic leadership and his commitment to fighting extremism position him as a valuable partner for global powers focused on counterterrorism. Under his leadership, Pakistan can continue to work with international intelligence agencies and security organizations to root out extremism, not only within its borders but across the region.

Global powers with security interests in South Asia and the Middle East would find in Khan an essential partner for maintaining peace, combating radicalization, and promoting tolerance. His balanced approach to governance, which seeks to address the root causes of extremism through education, economic opportunities, and social reforms, offers a sustainable solution to terrorism that benefits both Pakistan and the international community.

A Stable Pakistan: A Win-Win for everyone

Imran Khan's return to power presents a rare opportunity for global powers to partner with a Pakistan that is stable, prosperous, and committed to reform. His leadership promises a Pakistan that not only tackles its internal challenges but also contributes positively to the global order—whether through enhanced security, economic partnerships, or environmental cooperation.

For global powers, a stable Pakistan under Imran Khan is not just an advantage; it's a necessity in an increasingly interconnected world. Khan's leadership would bring about a new era of cooperation, mutual benefit, and shared prosperity, ensuring that Pakistan plays a pivotal role in the future of global geopolitics.

Moving Forward: Imran Khan-The Only and Last Hope to Make Pakistan a Great Country

In the midst of Pakistan's political and economic chaos, one man stands as a beacon of hope, a symbol of potential change: Imran Khan. His unwavering commitment to the nation, coupled with his integrity and vision for a better Pakistan, has made him the only viable leader capable of navigating the country out of its current crisis. With a unique combination of political leadership, celebrity status, and unshakable honesty, Imran Khan represents the possibility of restoring not only Pakistan's lost dignity but also its economic prosperity.

A Vision for a New Pakistan

Imran Khan's political journey began as an outsider, challenging the status quo of Pakistan's political elite. Unlike traditional politicians, whose careers have been built on corruption, nepotism, and manipulation, Imran Khan entered politics with a singular mission: to serve the people and create a nation where justice, fairness, and accountability reign. His vision was clear: a Pakistan that is free from the clutches of corruption, one that attracts foreign investment, creates opportunities for its youth, and upholds the values of democracy and equality.

Imran Khan's leadership is centered around the idea that Pakistan can rise again—through reform, discipline, and a return to meritocracy. Under his guidance, Pakistan can build institutions that are strong, transparent, and accountable to the people, paving the way for a thriving economy and a just society. His core message has always been one of self-reliance and the restoration of Pakistan's national pride. Imran Khan's idea of a "Naya Pakistan" goes beyond slogans; it is a call for a complete overhaul of the system that has failed the Pakistani people for decades.

The Power of Celebrity Status and Global Recognition

What sets Imran Khan apart from other leaders is not just his vision, but also his global stature. As a world-renowned cricketer, philanthropist, and social activist, Imran Khan commands respect and admiration not only within Pakistan but across the globe. His success in cricket—culminating in leading Pakistan to its first World Cup victory in 1992—cemented his place as a national hero. His subsequent work in philanthropy, including the founding of the Shaukat Khanum Memorial Cancer Hospital, further enhanced his reputation as a man of action, capable of turning his dreams into reality.

Imran Khan's celebrity status has granted him an unparalleled platform to rally support and influence change. His international fame gives him the ability to connect with global leaders, attract foreign investment, and bring attention to Pakistan's plight on the world stage. In a country where foreign investment is crucial for economic revival, Imran Khan's stature gives Pakistan the credibility it needs to rebuild its economy. He is not just a domestic politician but an internationally recognized figure who can inspire confidence in investors, diplomats, and international organizations.

In an era where global connectivity and the influence of media are at an all-time high, Imran Khan's celebrity status is an invaluable asset. He has the ability to engage with international leaders, organizations, and investors in a way that few other political figures can. Whether it's attracting foreign capital to Pakistan or advocating for the country's issues on the global stage, Imran Khan's recognition as a world-renowned figure puts him in a unique position to rebuild Pakistan's global standing.

Honesty and Integrity: A Rare Commodity in Pakistani Politics

Perhaps the most defining feature of Imran Khan's leadership is his unwavering commitment to honesty and integrity. In a political landscape dominated by corruption, where leaders are often seen as self-serving and disconnected from the needs of the people, Imran Khan stands out as a rare exception. His track record as an anti-corruption crusader and his personal commitment to leading by example have earned him the respect of millions of Pakistanis.

Imran Khan's honesty is not just a personal trait but a foundational principle of his political philosophy. He has consistently championed transparency and accountability, both in his personal life and in his political career. He has resisted the temptation of the political elite to engage in corrupt practices, and his party, Pakistan Tehreek-e-Insaf (PTI), has made anti-corruption a core tenet of its platform. His commitment to rooting out corruption within government institutions, despite facing intense opposition, has earned him both praise and criticism. But what is undeniable is that Imran Khan's integrity has become his most powerful weapon in winning the hearts and minds of the people.

In a country where corruption is so entrenched that it has become the norm rather than the exception, Imran Khan's commitment to honesty resonates deeply with ordinary citizens. His clean image and reputation for taking tough stances against corrupt practices have created a sense of hope among the people. Many Pakistanis see him as the only leader who can bring about the systemic changes necessary to eliminate corruption, rebuild the country's institutions, and restore public faith in the political process.

Imran Khan's Leadership: The Key to Investor Confidence

Pakistan's economic meltdown is largely due to the erosion of investor confidence, driven by years of political instability, corruption, and a lack of effective governance. Imran Khan has repeatedly emphasized the need for a business-friendly environment, transparency, and a corruption-free government in order to attract both domestic and foreign investment.

His ability to create such an environment is grounded in his leadership style, which prioritizes merit-based policies, a free-market economy, and an end to the culture of political patronage that has stifled entrepreneurship in the country. As a businessman himself, Imran Khan understands the importance of creating a conducive environment for investors, whether they are local or international. Under his leadership, Pakistan has the potential to become an investment hub in South Asia, with thriving industries, improved infrastructure, and a stable political climate that encourages foreign capital to flow into the country. Imran Khan's appeal to investors is not limited to his leadership qualities alone. His track record as a philanthropist and his demonstrated ability to fund and execute large-scale projects, such as the Shaukat Khanum Memorial Hospital, speaks to his credibility and capacity for turning ambitious ideas into tangible results. Investors are more likely to put their money in a country that is led by someone who is not only capable of leading but has also demonstrated a commitment to delivering on promises.

Moreover, his transparent approach to governance, his focus on reducing the role of the military in economic affairs, and his desire to streamline bureaucracy can help bring about the necessary reforms to restore Pakistan's economic stability. Imran Khan's administration would prioritize policies that encourage entrepreneurship, promote innovation, and create a favorable environment for businesses to flourish. With the right leadership, Pakistan can become a regional powerhouse.

Rebuilding Pakistan's Global Standing

Imran Khan's leadership could also restore Pakistan's standing on the global stage. The country has suffered from a perception problem, largely due to its unstable political environment, human rights issues, and strained international relations. Under Imran Khan, Pakistan can rebuild its diplomatic ties, particularly with neighboring countries and key global powers.

His foreign policy, which emphasizes peace, stability, and economic cooperation, contrasts sharply with the confrontational policies of previous governments. Imran Khan's focus on building strong bilateral relationships, improving Pakistan's image abroad, and engaging with international organizations in a constructive manner can help Pakistan secure vital aid, attract investment, and build meaningful partnerships that contribute to the country's long-term development.

Conclusion: Imran Khan as the Savior of Pakistan

In a country plagued by corruption, mismanagement, and political instability, Imran Khan offers a glimmer of hope. His vision for Pakistan, combined with his celebrity status, honesty, and commitment to reform, makes him the only leader capable of putting the country back on the path to prosperity. Imran Khan's unique ability to unite the people, attract foreign investment, and restore national pride is the solution that Pakistan desperately needs.

Moreover, Khan's resilience in the face of adversity, from surviving assassination attempts to standing tall against military and political conspiracies, has transformed him into a symbol of resistance. His unwavering fight for justice, accountability, and democracy has inspired millions, particularly the youth, to rally behind him. As Pakistan stands at a crossroads, Khan's leadership represents not just a return to stability but the promise of a Naya Pakistan—a nation that upholds the values of transparency, equality, and sovereignty in its truest form. For many, Imran Khan is not just a political leader, but the savior Pakistan has been waiting for.

Imran Khan is not only the ONLY HOPE for Pakistan, but he represents the last chance to reshape the nation's future, confront its deteriorating mindset, and restore the self-esteem of a people long shackled by systemic corruption, external influence, and a legacy of colonial-era subjugation. More than a political leader, Khan stands as a symbol of liberation from the *"Ghulaami"* (slavery) mindset inherited from the colonial era—a mindset that has long hindered Pakistan's progress, keeping it dependent on foreign powers and mired in a cycle of servitude.

Khan's leadership offers a path towards true independence, not just in terms of foreign policy, but also in how Pakistanis perceive themselves. He envisions a self-reliant nation that rejects the inferiority complex instilled during the colonial period, instead embracing a new era of dignity, self-worth, and national pride. His unwavering commitment to justice, accountability, and restoring the sovereignty of Pakistan has inspired millions to believe in the possibility of a brighter future.

By challenging the status quo and encouraging Pakistan to break free from its past, **Khan has the power to eliminate the "Ghulaam" mindset**, instilling a renewed sense of purpose and self-confidence in the people. His leadership has the potential to transform Pakistan's psyche, empowering it to rise above its colonial legacy and forge a future defined by honor, self-determination, and national pride. He is the only leader capable of unlocking this potential, making him the last true chance for Pakistan to fully reclaim its independence—both mentally and materially—and to chart its own course toward prosperity and global respect.

THE ROAD AHEAD WILL NOT BE EASY, AND THE CHALLENGES WILL BE IMMENSE. BUT WITH IMRAN KHAN AT THE HELM, PAKISTAN HAS A CHANCE TO RISE FROM THE ASHES OF ITS CURRENT CRISIS AND REBUILD ITSELF INTO A GREAT NATION—A NATION THAT CAN PROVIDE OPPORTUNITIES FOR ITS PEOPLE, RESTORE ITS DIGNITY ON THE GLOBAL STAGE, AND BECOME AN ECONOMIC POWERHOUSE IN THE REGION. IMRAN KHAN IS NOT JUST A POLITICAL LEADER; HE IS THE HOPE FOR A BRIGHTER, MORE PROSPEROUS PAKISTAN.

LONG LIVE PAKISTAN

www.ingramcontent.com/pod-product-compliance
Lightning Source LLC
Chambersburg PA
CBHW040037070726
47636CB00089B/686/J